CHILDREN AND CRIME

TO DAVID HOLMAN

CHILDREN
& CRIME

BOB HOLMAN

A LION BOOK

Published by
Lion Publishing plc
Sandy Lane West, Oxford, England
ISBN 0 7459 3121 9
Albatross Books Pty Ltd
PO Box 320, Sutherland, NSW 2232, Australia
ISBN 0 7324 1307 9

First edition 1995
10 9 8 7 6 5 4 3 2 1

Acknowledgments
Thanks to the following copyright holders for permission to use
extracts. Every effort has been made to trace copyright holders, and
we apologize if there are any inadvertent omissions or errors in the
acknowledgments.
Families of Courage, published by ATD Fourth World.
Gaskin, by G. Gaskin with J. Macveigh, published by Jonathan Cape.
No Cake, No Jam: A War-time Childhood, Marian Hughes, published by
William Heinemann Ltd, by permission of Reed Consumer Books.
A Place Called Hope, by Tom O'Neill, published by Basil Blackwell.
'A Friend in Need' by S. Mapp, republished by permission of the
editor, *Community Care*.
© *The Guardian* for permission to use extracts from the following: M.
Bunting, 'Parents on the front line'; C. Irvine, 'Diary'; B. Holman,
'Diary'; A. Shearer, 'Finding the way home'; A. Phillips, 'Small steps in
the right direction'.
© *The Observer* for permission to use extracts from: D. Rose. 'The
messy truth about Britain's violent youth'.
Thanks to the Family Policy Studies Centre for the use of the table by
Schweinhart and Weikart (1993) as reproduced in Utting *et al* in *Crime
and the Family: Improving child-rearing and preventing delinquency*, 1993.
The author's interviews with staff and users at the Walcot Centre in
Chapter 7 first appeared in *Putting Families First*, published by
Macmillan Press Ltd, 1987.

CONTENTS

Preface   6

Part One: Analysis

1   Cause for Concern   10

2   Crime and the Family   22

3   Not Just the Family   41

4   The Crime of Poverty   54

5   What They Say   78

Part Two: Action

6   Prevention Before Punishment   94

7   Laying the Foundations—the Early Years   108

8   Alongside the Vulnerable—Help for Parents   130

9   Something for Youngsters—Youth Work   152

10 Resourceful Friends—Befriending Young People   174

11 Proclamation   204

    Bibliography   219

    Index   222

Preface

Juvenile crime: why do they do it? How can we prevent it? Delinquency is a worrying and complex subject. I do not possess all the answers but in this book I shall attempt to throw some light on it by drawing upon both personal examples and academic studies.

Both my own practical experience and references to written studies are drawn upon here because they reflect my life. My early educational progress was not promising. As I recount in *The Evacuation: A Very British Revolution* (Lion Publishing, 1995), I was a war-time evacuee who missed much schooling. I failed the 11 plus examination but succeeded on being given a second chance when a secondary modern school was changed into a grammar school. I struggled there but passed exams, due to the individual interest of a number of dedicated teachers who had the ability both to discipline and teach. Then one asked me if I would be applying to university. I did not know what a university was for and, apart from the teachers, I had never met anyone who had attended. But I went and followed the same pattern of initially being out of my depth and then enjoying it.

After five years at university, I became a child care officer in a local authority children's department. I had moved from the academic to the practical life. I worked with what were then called deprived children, as well as delinquent ones. Our corporation house was in the midst of my working patch, I was married, I seemed set for a career in social work. Then I received a hand-written letter from Professor Richard Titmuss at the London School of Economics, suggesting that I apply for an assistant lectureship. To say I was astonished is to put it mildly, for I did not think he had even noticed me. But I did as he recommended. From practice to academic.

For the next eleven years I enjoyed teaching and researching in three universities. Yet, with time, I became aware of an unease. I felt academia was too remote from practice. How could the lessons from research be applied? And if I was teaching social work skills to students, should I not also be exercising them outside? I finished up as a professor and, to be frank, not a very competent one. Administration and committee meetings were not my strong points. Above all, I found Christian conviction taking a stronger hold on my life. Jesus was not a distant teacher. His example was that of the involved mixer. Whatever the reasons, I felt constrained to move. Academic to practitioner.

For the following decade, I worked with a community project, sponsored by the Church of England Children's Society, on the Southdown estate on the edge of Bath. My greatest friend and later colleague was Dave Wiles, himself a former delinquent. The project was based on our home, and many potential and actual delinquent youngsters passed through its doors, some of whom emerge in the pages of this book. When the project was fully in the hands of local residents, we moved to my wife's native Glasgow where we have spent the last eight years in Easterhouse. I have come into contact with many families struggling bravely in adverse circumstances. I have spent time with youngsters who have resisted the temptations of crime and those who have succumbed. Both have lessons to teach us.

My intention, then, is to use experience and academic study to explore the subject of children and crime. The book will look at the nature of crime, explanations of delinquency, means to combat it and, above all, ways of preventing it. The book is not written for academics or professional experts. It is aimed at the concerned, ordinary citizen, those who want to be involved in helping young offenders and in reducing delinquency. It is for those people who want to use their own abilities within the context of their churches, youth clubs, community associations, and other voluntary organizations. It is for residents who may lack formal qualifications but who do possess attitudes and skills which can play a part in combating a serious social problem. I am convinced that, in the long run, the main means of preventing juvenile crime rests with caring families within strong communities.

As with most authors, I want to thank others. The idea of this book originated with my editor, Maurice Lyon, who always gives encouragement. Then, going back to my own teens, I want to acknowledge my debt to David Dalton and the late Tom Anders. In the late 1940s, they had a vision to run Christian youth clubs for the kind of youngsters who had nothing to do with church. They started in the park near my home by putting down some cricket gear and walking away. Once children started playing, they joined in. A club was established. They gave me much individual attention and were long-suffering towards my bad behaviour. Recently, David Dalton told me that on one occasion they had concluded, reluctantly, that they had had enough and that I should be kicked out of the club. Tom was deputed to inform me but, when it came to it, he had not the heart to do so. I hope that some of their patient individual concern, within a framework of youth activities, has rubbed off on me.

Lastly, my family. My wife Annette, daughter Ruth and son-in-law Bruce are a joy. But especially I wish to thank our son David. His childhood years were mainly spent in a home which was a project. He shared it with scores of other children and never complained. He was alongside a number of delinquents yet never became one himself. After graduating, he worked with young people with special needs and now he is an academic. I am very proud of him and I dedicate this book to him.

Bob Holman
Glasgow, May 1995

PART ONE

ANALYSIS

CHAPTER

ONE

Cause for Concern

Since 25 November last year, the day when the faces
of Robert Thompson and Jon Venables, the killers of
James Bulger, looked out from the front pages of
every newspaper in Britain, the press has devoted
hundreds of pages and thousands of words to
attempts at answering the questions How? and Why?
Oliver James, Harper & Queens, May 1994

Juvenile offenders are an emotive issue. There is a small
group of highly disturbed and damaged young people
who wreak havoc: children who have stolen up to 100
cars, raided 23 stores in a night, even one fourteen-year-
old who claims to have committed 1,000 burglaries in
two years.
The Guardian, 16 May 1994

This week 400,000 sixteen-year-olds leave school. A
quarter are likely to join the 100,000 who left school last
year and have never worked. How will they pass the long
summer evenings? Practising making petrol bombs,
quite likely.

Newcastle, Cardiff, Manchester, Bristol, Birmingham, Oxford, Stockton, Luton, Burnley, Blackburn,
Huddersfield, the roll call of riots grows daily. Speak

to any community worker or policeman on any estate in the country and hear the same reply—it could be us next time.
Barry Hugill, The Observer, 26 July 1992

There are many in our society who live in daily fear of such thieves and thugs. Old people who dare not answer their doors at night. Weak and vulnerable people who find it an ordeal to venture out into the street.
Daily Mail, 14 May 1994

The tragic murder of two-year-old James Bulger by two eleven-year-old boys shocked a nation already well used to media coverage of juvenile crime. Popular newspapers suggest that an escalating crime rate is out of control. The young criminals range from youthful murderers to teenagers who are almost professional thieves and to hooligans who hunt in packs and who steal cars for dangerous joy-riding.

Crime by young people is a cause for concern. I write as one who has been the victim of crimes, as the following incidents show:

We were at camp in Norfolk when I received a message from a boy's mother with the terrible news that his dad had died suddenly. She asked me not to tell him until I brought him home.

On the day we returned, I first took the young boy to our home to dump our luggage. The back door was smashed in: our home had been turned over. The TV, ornaments, valuables, clocks, had been stolen. Other items were smashed. The combination of having to tell the boy of his dad's death and the impact of the burglary was almost too much for me. Later it was established that the break-in was by local teenagers who knew we were away.

Another time a mother and her grown-up son and daughter came in distress to ask me to drive them to hospital where another son was seriously injured. I agreed immediately. Later I discovered that my wallet was missing from our flat. I tackled the mother and it emerged that her son had lifted it. Then he came to explain. He had borrowed money from a loan shark to buy supplies for his children. He showed me his knee, smashed in by a baseball bat wielded by the shark's thugs when he could not repay the high interest rates. He stole from me in order to avoid another beating.

At 2 a.m. one morning I was woken by a banging on the door. A young man stood there, dishevelled and wide-eyed. He asked for and then demanded money. Knowing that he wanted it for drugs, I refused. He continued to argue, saying that if he did not pay the drug dealers, they would attack him. As his anger rose, he accused me of not caring. He swore and raged that Christians like me should be ready to help others. Then he produced a meat cleaver to threaten me. After what seemed an age, I persuaded him to go. A few minutes later, I descended the stairs of the close to make sure the bottom door was closed. I was shaking and sweating. Later that night, he was arrested by the police for another attempted crime.

Another night at 7.30 p.m. children were playing in the street. Suddenly there were shouts and screams outside a bottom flat. A nineteen-year-old male lay dead from stab wounds. A seventeen-year-old was critically injured. Subsequently, two teenagers were charged with murder.

Faced with crime, I have felt anger that my home and my family should be the victims; resentment that someone I was trying to help should steal from me; fear that I would be attacked; and deep sorrow that youngsters I knew had been killed and maimed. The incidents also provoked in me feelings I hardly like to admit—a desire for revenge and for harsh punishment to be inflicted. In addition to experiencing crime directed against my friends, neighbours, family and self, I have, in my years in youth and neighbourhood work, known a number of offenders, have attended juvenile courts and children's hearings,

have visited young people in penal institutions. I hope
that this breadth of experience will be useful in discussing
both the reasons for juvenile crime—or delinquency, as it
is called—and also the responses that we can make to it.

The nature of crime

The term juveniles is usually applied to children aged ten
to seventeen, while that of young adults is applied to those
aged seventeen to twenty. Sometimes a further distinction
is made, with fourteen- to seventeen-year-olds called young
persons. Here the terms will be used interchangeably. In
England and Wales, ten- to seventeen-year-olds can be
brought before youth courts which are still frequently
referred to by their old name of juvenile courts. In
Scotland, children are referred to an official called a
Reporter who then decides whether they should appear
before a Children's Hearing. The courts and hearings have
various means of dealing with those who come before them
according to their age, the nature of the offence, their
home circumstances and what seems to be in their best
interests. In the courts these means include an absolute
discharge, a fine, a supervision order, a probation order, a
community service order and detention in a young
offenders' institution. A children's hearing may discharge a
child without taking any action, make a home supervision
order, make a residential supervision order or suggest help
from a voluntary source.

What then are the main features of the offenders and
their offences?

Juvenile crime cannot be viewed in isolation from adult crime

After all, adult offenders were once children. In 1992,
the police recorded 5.6 million offences in England
and Wales and a further 600,000 in Scotland. Over the
past twenty-five years, these numbers have risen by

about 5 per cent a year, although for 1992–93 they fell by 1 per cent. Property crime—the most common offence—fraud and theft all decreased. However, violent crimes, which make up around 5 per cent of the total, rape, robbery and trafficking in controlled drugs continued to climb.

Crime is most commonly undertaken by males and particularly young males

Over 80 per cent of offenders are men, while 46 per cent of all offenders are under twenty-one years of age. It must be added that, although men predominate in the figures, this does not mean that the majority of males are criminals. A follow-up study of men born in 1953 found that, by the age of thirty-five, 65 per cent had no convictions of any kind. Females commit only a minority of known crimes with a particularly low incidence for offences such as burglary, sexual assault and violence. The low numbers occur both amongst adults and juveniles although there is now a slight increase amongst the latter. Oddly enough, the small incidence may mean that programmes for dealing with female offenders are not well developed and there are some indications that females may be treated more severely by the courts.

What of ethnic minorities?

Black young people may be over-represented in crime figures. They made up 12 per cent of all those aged fourteen to twenty years serving custodial sentences in January 1991. But there are important variations: those from Indian, Pakistani and Bangladeshi backgrounds have very low numbers while those from African/West Indian backgrounds feature more highly. Philip Rosser, who has studied ethnic crime, suggests that the latter are more liable to detection and prosecution because of 'racial prejudice amongst the police; greater "visibility";

stereotypical impressions that black people will act more unlawfully than white people' (P. Rosser, see bibliography). The authorities are aware of the problem and the Criminal Justice Act of 1991 states that persons involved in justice now have a duty to 'avoid discriminating against any person on the ground of race or sex'. It should in addition be mentioned that Afro-Caribbeans also have a greater chance of being the victims of crime.

A rising crime rate?

The media often give the impression that crime rates amongst the young are on a constant and rapid ascent. Yet the following official statistics reveal a different picture:

Table 1

Juveniles (left) and young adults found guilty or cautioned for indictable offences 1981–93

1981	174,300	132,800
1989	99,300	115,100
1991	105,000	129,800
1992	110,400	130,400
1993	129,500	90,500

Criminal Statistics, England and Wales 1992

It can be seen that although the 1993 figures showed an increase for juveniles as compared with the previous year, those for young adults fell. Moreover both groups reveal a considerable drop from the early 1980s. In Scotland, the number of children referred to Reporters reached a peak of 24,941 in 1991. However, of these only 35 per cent were then brought before a children's hearing and of these only a third had actually committed an offence. The rise in Scottish figures appears mainly due to an increase in non-offence cases, that is, children brought before hearings because they may be lacking proper parental care, as in instances of those against whom sexual abuse is inflicted.

A falling crime rate?

The reduction, or at least the slowing down of delinquency rates is to be welcomed but it must be put in a context of a drop in the total number of children in the population, in the probability that the police informally caution numbers of offenders, and in the knowledge that it is not known who commits many unsolved crimes.

A life of crime?

The majority of young offenders do not turn into hardened, adult criminals. But fears are expressed about a core of children who repeatedly offend and seem set for a life of crime.

Why worry?

Britain is not about to be overrun by an explosion of juvenile crime. Most people are not daily confronted by muggings and break-ins. So why be concerned?

First, because the around 220,000 youngsters who do annually commit offences make up a large number. Further, even though the overall crime rate has shown a slight decline, more serious crimes, such as those associated with violence, continue to climb.

Second, because crime is costly. Shops lose about £2million annually through shoplifting while individuals lose a similar amount through theft. The cost of vandalism to public buildings such as schools runs into millions of pounds. Further, in 1992–93, over £9 billion had to be spent on running the police, the courts, the probation service and other parts of the criminal justice system. These costs are handed on to the public through higher prices in the shops, increased insurance premiums and higher taxes.

Third, crime can have terrible effects on the victims. An elderly friend of mine opened her door to a hooded figure who, armed with a knife, demanded money. The effect of that trauma stayed with her for months. A nineteen-year-old was set about by a gang, knocked down, kicked and had a broken bottle thrust into his face. His wounds required multiple stitching and he will carry the scars for the rest of his life. On Christmas Day, a woman walking across some waste land in our estate was attacked, dragged down, and sexually assaulted by two boys. The horrifying experience will haunt her. Even worse is the long-term grief and despair of the parents of murdered children. If for nothing else, crime must be tackled in order to reduce the emotional, psychological, physical and material sufferings of the victims.

Fourth, crime spoils its perpetrators. I think of some lively boys who played in our youth club football teams and enjoyed the open-air holidays. Now a few of them are embittered, unemployed teenagers who break into houses. I think of a young man who often dropped in for a chat, who amused us with his sense of humour, and who displayed a real skill when tinkering with motor bikes. Now he is in and out of prison. I think of a teenager who was full of warmth and good at looking after smaller children. Yet she could never resist theft and fraud. I sat in court and watched as she was sent down. Their potential is unfulfilled, their character warped, their lives spoilt and, in some cases, their freedom removed. Crime must be tackled to prevent the waste, even destruction, of these lives.

It is as well to be open about my own Christian foundations. I believe that the world was created by God and that Christians have a responsibility to try to ensure that it is not ruined by injustices. I believe that all people are of infinite and equal value to God. It follows that we have a duty to protect them from the attacks of criminals. Yet even criminals are God's beings. Jesus Christ was crucified between two bandits and, in his agony, still had time to listen to and forgive one of them. In like manner, I reckon that Christians today must have a concern for those considered most unworthy by society.

Of course, followers of other religions can argue a similar concern. Humanists can reason that a common humanity is a sufficient basis for concerted action. Whatever our particular motivation, I believe that collectively we should strive for a reduction of crime, the protection of citizens, and for the redemption of potential and actual offenders.

Analysis and action

A case has been made for action against youth crime. But effective action can only follow informed analysis. What are the explanations for juvenile offending? A start can be made by disposing of some statements often made in churches and pubs—not necessarily by the same people!

'It's all due to sin'

Sometimes church-goers state that crime is due to sin and that delinquents will never reform until converted. Certainly, crime is one manifestation of sin. But not all sinners become criminals. The question is, why do some commit illegal offences such as stealing while others major on the legal sins of hypocrisy, pride, arrogance, the worship of money, gossip and so on? Further, it must be admitted that some offenders, including many juvenile ones, do cease criminal activities without dramatic spiritual experiences. This is not to deny that Christian conversion can have a dramatic impact on personal behaviour. The point is rather that the explanation of crime is more complicated than a parrot-like repeating of, 'It's all due to sin.'

'It's in the blood'

As an Agatha Christie fan, I've noticed how often she attributes crime to inherited biological factors. Thus her

Archdeacon Brabazon explains the apparently murderous action of a talented young man to 'some small deformity of a chromosome or gene'. The view persists. 'Don't waste your time on that one,' I was advised concerning a young tearaway. 'His dad was a jail-bird and he'll be the same. It's in the blood.'

Needless to say, there is no blood group or gene which can be identified with criminality. With more sophistication, writers like Hans Eysenck argue that certain inherited traits, such as aggressiveness or impulsiveness, do direct people into crime. Leaving aside the disputed question of whether such characteristics are biologically inherited, this approach does not explain why some use their aggression to become not criminals but successful boxers, salespersons or politicians. Nor does it explain why many young offenders are passive and withdrawn rather than aggressive and impulsive. Significantly, a Danish study of 14,000 adoptees—children removed from their natural parents soon after birth—found that those whose parents had committed violent offences were not more likely to do so than those whose parents were not criminals. Inherited traits may influence behaviour but they are not decisive and their development depends on the external factors with which they interact.

'I blame the welfare state'

During the 1970s and 80s, state welfare was subjected to much criticism from politicians and writers known as the New Right. In 1971, Rhodes Boyson, who later became a government minister, complained that the welfare state led to a decline in personal responsibility and the promotion of fecklessness. More recently, the theme has been taken up by an American right-wing guru, Charles Murray, who has visited Britain on a number of occasions. He claimed that council estates were being taken over by a criminal underclass made up of 'young, healthy, low-income males [who] choose not to take jobs' and by young women who choose to have babies outside marriage. The connection between single mothers and delinquency will be dealt with in the next chapter. The young men, Murray asserted, could choose to laze around because of the availability of generous state benefits. However, the meaninglessness of life without work made many turn to drugs. Next, he continued, 'The cost of drugs makes crime the only feasible way to make money to pay for them.' Hence, according to this view, estates and inner cities became awash with unemployment and crime. Murray and his supporters succeeded in convincing many that state welfare and crime went together and was in contrast with the free-market Victorian era when there was less crime. And so the popular cry, 'I blame the welfare state.'

Blaming crime on to state welfare does not stand up to serious examination. In my book *A New Deal for Social Welfare*, I explained that, although some estates did experience a high level of crime, they were not being overtaken by a criminal underclass and that they contained many residents (often unemployed themselves) who were strongly opposed to crime and drug-taking. I also drew upon recent surveys to show that, far from being contented with the dole, most unemployed people wanted work, stable family lives and safe communities. Any escalation of crime cannot be blamed on the welfare state.

The point can also be made by looking at pre-welfare Britain. The historian Professor Neale in his book *Bath: a Social History* recounts that in fashionable Bath of the eighteenth and nineteenth centuries, levels of violence were extremely high while some streets were taken over by 'thieves, prostitutes, gamblers, juvenile delinquents, vagrants and the destitute.' In less fashionable but more industrial Glasgow, violence, including murder, was frequent with, at times, gangs such as the Penny Mob gang wielding more power than the police. A Britain without state welfare may have meant comfortable, safe lives for the very prosperous but for many it meant lives shortened by poverty and crime. Indeed, Christian politicians like George Lansbury saw the establishment of the welfare state as a means of improving social conditions and public values in order to reduce crime. The fact is that crime, including juvenile delinquency, has existed before, during and now after the welfare state.

Crime cannot be accounted for by generalizations about sin, genes and welfare. The explanations are far more profound and varied. With particular reference to young people, this book will investigate the influence of the family, the media, prevailing values, and social deprivations. It will seek the views of experts, practitioners, and the delinquents themselves. This will be followed by suggestions and examples, some of which come from my own experiences, of how to prevent juvenile crime. My proposals are not addressed to professional workers and academics but to citizens who may live in areas where crime rates are high, to ordinary people who participate in voluntary organizations, community groups, and churches.

The understanding of crime is not an exact science. Readers should not expect that social science can identify causation in the way that medical science can pin down the cause of pneumonia. The interaction between individuals and society is too complex for that. Analysing the reasons for and suggesting means of modifying delinquency is more akin to understanding football. The astute manager can study his team as individuals and as a group, he can perceive the state of opponents, he can recommend certain tactics. But he is not sure of winning and certainly cannot always predict the outcomes—after all, not even football managers win the pools. In like manner, a study of criminal behaviour can lead not to certainty but rather to the identification of patterns and trends. From these some proposals can be made which may be useful today in tackling delinquency.

TWO

Crime and the Family

The family has long been blamed for juvenile delinquency. The rising crime rate in the early 1940s was attributed to the breaking up of family life as a result of the Second World War. In 1958, an MP speaking in the Commons, condemned 'parents, indifferent to their children and utterly without social conscience'. Of late, the horrible murder of James Bulger has sparked off renewed claims that the unit of the family is being destroyed with the outcome of violence and other crimes.

What is the family? In Western society it is usually regarded as a unit made up of parent(s) and dependent children, born to one or both of the parents, residing together in the same household.

Is there a link between family life and delinquency? Certainly. An authoritative review of the research undertaken for the Family Policies Study Centre by David Utting and his colleagues concluded that 'the tangled roots of delinquency lie, to a considerable extent, inside the family.'

The family is at the root of delinquency. Family experiences are also blamed for causing mental illness, child abuse and sexual crimes. In 1967, the Reith lecturer Edmund Leach stated, 'Far from being the basis of the good society, the family with its narrow privacy and tawdry secrets is the source of all our discontents.' In the face of such criticisms, efforts have been made to abolish the family, particularly in China and the former USSR, and to replace it by systems in which the care of children rests less with their biological parents and more with professional carers. Further, in attempts to move away from the traditional model of a married couple staying together for life and accepting responsibility for their children, experiments have taken place with communes, serial marriage and open marriage. Yet the nuclear or small family unit has still survived.

The family may be a cause of delinquency yet, paradoxically, so is the lack of a family. In 1994 Robert Black was sentenced to ten life-terms after assaulting and murdering a number of small children. Black was an evil man who had to be imprisoned in order to ensure the safety of children. But what was his upbringing like? He was the illegitimate son of a factory worker. He never knew his father and his mother soon placed him in a foster home. His substitute parents died when he was ten and he ended up in a children's home. Here he was systematically sexually abused by a member of staff. At the age of sixteen, soon after leaving the home, Black was convicted of his first sexual offence. Before long he was in a Borstal for offences against a small girl. Once released, his offending multiplied and reached at least seventy in number. Black suffered from a lack of a stable, affectionate family. Institutional care exposed him to sexual abuse which appeared to shape the way he then behaved towards others. It was not family life but a lack of it which moulded Black's warped personality.

The fact is that the family can be a source of good or ill, for it is within the family that parents find happiness or distress and it is within the family that children have, or do not have, their essential needs met. The family is the major means of the socialization of children; that is, where they can be taught ideas of right and wrong, where they can learn the limits of tolerated behaviour, where they can acquire the skills, knowledge and attitudes to live as adults. Not least, it is within the family that children can gain an identity for themselves, can perceive themselves as good or bad, liked or unliked.

The family can be overemphasized to the point of becoming an idol. In the USA, Rodney Clapp, himself an evangelical leader, explains that fundamentalists of the moral majority persuasion claim the nuclear family, capitalism and nationalism to be not only the rightful foundations of their country but also derived from the Bible. Clapp disagrees on all counts but here it is sufficient to pick out just two points he makes about the family. One is that, in making the family into an idol, its worshippers tend to cut their children off from other useful and good societal institutions such as neighbourhood groups, the extended family, persons from different classes and cultures, and welfare services. The other is that, in the Bible the families of the Israelites tended to be extensive households quite unlike the contemporary insular, small and private families in Western society.

My own view is that today's family unit is to be supported by Christians not because its identikit can be found in the Bible, but because it is an institution which can convey certain virtues, such as stability, fidelity, compassion, responsibility and permanency, which most certainly are encouraged in the Bible. Further, like Clapp, I hold that the family should not be coccooned from the rest of society but should be integrated into and supported by it. After all, the New Testament both upholds the mutual obligations of parents and children and also teaches that we should love our neighbours— that is, people outside the family. Of course, it is not just Christians. Many, probably most, citizens in Britain, whether Christian or not, would agree that the family unit—made up of parents and dependent children—is more likely to convey positive care and relationships than other large-scale forms of child care where natural parents are absent.

Mothers and fathers

So the family unit is central to the theme of this book. There will be no suggestions that it should be abolished or weakened. Family life has the potential to develop stable, honest and happy children yet, paradoxically, can also stimulate dishonesty and maladjustment. The next step, then, is to identify those practices and attitudes of parents which do have negative effects on their children. But which parent?

Most attention has been focussed on the role of mothers. John Bowlby is probably the best-known figure in British child psychiatry. His interest in juvenile delinquency arose in his pre-war clinic where he observed that young criminals had frequently experienced unsatisfactory relationships with their mothers or had often been separated from them. He identified mothers who were cold towards, even rejecting of, their babies, who could not easily express affection, who never made strong bonds with their children, who allowed them often to be cared for by others. The results of such mothering, Bowlby argued, were children marked by egotism, sexual misdemeanours, persistent stealing and violence. After the war, Bowlby reviewed a number of studies in his best-selling book *Child Care and the Growth of Love*. In it occurs his much-quoted advice that it was essential for an infant to experience 'a warm, intimate and continuous relationship with his mother (or mother substitute) in which both find satisfaction and enjoyment'.

Bowlby's findings have been debated, clarified and refined. Arguments continue as to just what behaviour does make up good mothering, as to just what age is the most vital for a lack of it (the first, second or third years of life), and as to whether the initial ill-effects of poor mothering can later be reversed. But there is general agreement that infants do suffer if their mothers fail to supply not just food and shelter but also the emotional vitamins of love and affection expressed in cuddling, attention, approval and stimulation. The child care historian Jean Heywood commented that the studies of Bowlby and his colleagues had explained why so many deprived children were eventually found in 'prisons and mental wards of hospitals' and also taught that growing up themselves as adults unable to express love and affection, they 'produce another generation of neglected or delinquent or maladjusted boys and girls'.

Bowlby and many of his followers concentrated on mothers. A few later researchers have also stressed the part played by fathers in child rearing. Not long after Bowlby, a study by Robert Andry compared the fathers of delinquent boys aged eleven to fifteen years old with those of non-delinquents. He found that the former participated less with their sons in every way, spoke less, played less, were present less. The boys felt they could look to their fathers neither for guidance nor for comfort and consequently tended to act out their problems outside the homes in the form of delinquency.

Inadequate child care

Clearly both mothers and fathers are crucial in the way in which children's characters develop. From a number of long-term research studies of children, particularly those by Donald West and David Farrington in South London and Israel Kolvin in Newcastle, it is possible to identify some features of inadequate parenting, by both or one parent, which appear to be associated with delinquent behaviour in children.

Lack of a warm relationship

If babies are not given consistent warm love, conveyed both by physical touch and attitudes, there is a danger that they, later, become unable to love and be loved. Consequently, they are unable to make satisfactory relationships with other members of society.

Lack of stimulation

Children's abilities to form social and intellectual skills are held back if parents do not consistently encourage them to play and, at best, to play with them. A lack of such skills can hold children back at school; this may be compounded if the parents take little interest in their schooling. Children who do badly at school are more likely to become delinquent.

Lack of attention

Parents may neglect to feed their children properly. But there are other kinds of neglect or lack of attention. For instance, they may not give sufficient attention to problems like bullying within the home. Outside the home, they may neglect to monitor just what their children are doing or with whom they are mixing. The children thus may acquire habits and friends which later mean trouble.

Lack of discipline

Children do not benefit from harsh or inconsistent discipline. They do need firm discipline within a context of love. For without consistent discipline they do not learn when and how their behaviour is to be controlled, do not learn what is right and wrong.

Lack of example

Children model much of their behaviour and attitudes on those of their parents. Children of criminals are more likely than other children to become offenders themselves, not because they inherit some criminal gene but because they copy and take on the values held and practised by their parents.

Lack of permanence

All children, even when young, spend some time away from parents. Indeed, such separations are a step towards independence. However, if disruptions frequently occur which are not planned and do not provide loving carers but happen in erratic and unexpected ways following arguments with, say, one parent storming off in anger for a few days (or longer), or with arrangements having hastily and dramatically to be made for the children, then the effects can be negative. The children experience family life as unstable and such instability can then become a feature of their lives.

The child psychologist Dr Kellmer Pringle explained that children have four basic needs: for love and security, for praise and recognition, for new experiences, and for responsibility. If these needs are met, the children have the prospect of growing into young people whose emotions, skills and values enable them to relate satisfactorily with other individuals and to fit into society at large. If, on the other hand, they experience the kind of parenting identified above, then their needs will not be met and they may well develop into the types of people who:

- ◆ have difficulties in making personal relationships;

- ◆ cannot control their emotions;

- ◆ lack the skills and motivation to make the most of their abilities at school;

- ◆ have a sense of right and wrong out of keeping with dominant values.

In short, they become candidates for delinquency and for other behaviour which is unacceptable to society.

Some examples

Drawing upon my own experience, I will give examples of a couple of such children.

Doreen

'Are you in charge of this young lady, sir?' The store detective was icily polite. I nodded. Doreen, a fourteen-year-old, stood aggressively at his side. I'd gone to town to buy some equipment for the youth club and Doreen had come for the ride. She was suspended from school for spitting at a teacher and her mum had asked me to take her off her hands for a couple of hours. While I was selecting some games, she had slipped away and helped herself to some gloves, only to be apprehended by the detective. Red-faced, I followed him up the stairs to the manager's office. After much persuasion, the manager agreed to let her off with a warning and a promise from Doreen that she would not return. The warning did not have much effect. Five years later she was imprisoned for persistent shoplifting.

How did it come about? Doreen had never known her real dad, who had deserted the family when she was a few weeks old. Her mum provided the basics of food, clothes and shelter but rarely gave her cuddles and never seemed to have the time to read her stories. Later she told Doreen not to play truant but never attended the parents' evenings at the school. She warned Doreen about men yet had three co-habitees during Doreen's childhood. To be fair, Doreen did possess some attractive qualities. She could chat easily, be polite, offer to help. Yet she possessed no self-confidence, was easily offended, flared up and reacted aggressively when frustrated. She longed for affection, yet seemed to regard herself as worthless. Probably her upbringing had stimulated traits and behaviour which continually brought her into conflict with people in authority.

Daniel

Daniel lived a few streets from me. His mum was an attractive woman and deeply in love with her husband who had left the home for another woman. Sometimes he would return and she would accept him in every way until he left again. She remained faithful despite all the emotional and physical blows he gave her.

She really loved Daniel and, when he got into trouble, she would defend him to the full. Yet she was rarely able to communicate with him except by nagging and buying him things. Although living on Social Security, she would save to buy him expensive trainers, yet she also allowed him to stay out to all hours.

Daniel would often appear at our youth clubs. His jutting, belligerent face, his foul language and his readiness to resort to violence earned him a bad reputation. Yet at times he displayed a charm and an ability to talk his way out of tricky situations.

One year, he accompanied the junior club to camp. What a pain. The boys were required to do certain duties; to keep their tent clean, to wash up, to dry their clothes. Daniel just refused and, if other boys objected, he would hurl himself at them, kicking and punching. When adults intervened, he argued fiercely, kicked their shins, and ran off screaming that he was not coming back. When he did return, he sometimes then went through a period of calm. On the trip home, he got so wild and violent that he had to be forcibly held down in the minibus until we reached his address. His mother expressed little surprise or concern and just murmured weakly that the holiday must have got on top of him.

And so it continued. He went with the club to a sports rally where he was obviously looking for trouble. I had to return some goods he stole from a stall. He disrupted games and picked fights. Eventually, he persuaded another boy to run off with him in order to hitch-hike. We were miles from home so I had to intervene. I called them back, the other boy returned but Daniel dashed away. I chased, caught him and dragged him back. As I did so, a leather-clad heavy figure on a motor bike stopped and told me that if I wanted a fight I should pick on him, not on a kid. Fortunately, my colleague arrived to explain. We decided to take him home. Once in his house, Daniel stormed through, ignored his mum, and disappeared out of the back door. Mum smiled sadly, 'I can't imagine what has got into him.'

His mum was pleased that Daniel attended the clubs but she never accompanied him to the parents' nights or other joint activities. When I called to discuss his behaviour she could only complain that 'he gets picked on.' At one group, Daniel became frustrated at his attempts to make a radio. He lunged at another boy with a soldering iron and charged into another room to spoil a snooker game by sweeping the balls off the table. I took him home where his mother told him to sit down. He swore, leapt through an open window, seized a garden fork and attacked me with it. I struggled and disarmed him, whereupon he tore down the path hurling stones at the minibus and threatening to smash every window in my home. Mum said, 'Let him go. He's all right really.' A few days later, he knocked at my door as if nothing had happened and asked if we wanted his mum to wash the team's football shirts.

I tried to talk seriously with Daniel but he found difficulty in concentrating on subjects about himself. He would not contribute except to blame others. His mum loved him but had never exerted control, and so Daniel had never learned to control himself. His dad had been absent for much of his childhood and so never constituted an example of proper behaviour and attitudes on which the boy could model himself. As he grew older, Daniel was increasingly drawn into delinquency. The crimes multiplied in number and seriousness and, as a young adult, he served custodial sentences. I last saw him just before he was due to face another charge. We chatted in the street and he said, to my amazement, 'Remember that camp, Bob? That was great.' At his trial, he was sent to prison.

The above two cases concern children from low-income families and the connection between crime and poverty will be explored in a later chapter. Here it must be said that many low-income parents do care for their children in excellent fashion. They would regard as callous the practice of some wealthy parents who foist the responsibility of looking after their children on to nannies or private boarding schools. Inadequate parenting can occur in all social classes. In 1993, Verona in Italy was shocked by violent murders carried out by young men who showed no remorse but rather gloried in their crimes. The young men all came from homes of excessive wealth. Their parents had given them everything in materialistic terms—money, holidays, cars—but little else. Their sons tried murder for the kicks it gave them, for life seemed to have no meaning beyond immediate satisfaction. Perhaps the greatest failure of parents, whatever their social status, is to leave their children without a moral code, without values, without a sense that life is nothing more than individual gratification.

Broken families

Any consideration of the relationship between delinquency and family life inevitably turns to three topics—working mothers, divorced parents and single parenthood.

During the Second World War, many day nurseries were opened in Britain where mothers could leave their children in order to work for the war effort. After the war, many of the nurseries were closed down amidst the argument that the mothers of young children should not take employment, for to do so was to endanger their development. Today this argument still persists and is strongly put forward by some religious organizations in the USA who believe that mothers should stay at home as long as their children are still at school.

What does research show? The findings are complicated. The famous study of over 400 children by West and Farrington found that having a working mother was not related to later delinquency. Another study, cited by David Utting in his review of the research, noted that a mother's full-time employment did increase the risk of anti-social behaviour (not necessarily delinquency) amongst young children. Yet it also found that some mothers became so depressed at having to stay at home that this factor adversely affected their child care. At the risk of over-simplification, the upshot appears three-fold.

First, infants do need, as Bowlby showed, the continuous, close, attention of one of their parents (mother or father). Second, once the infant stage is passed, family life can actually benefit by parents working as it may bring in much-needed income and satisfaction and fulfilment for the parents. Third, these benefits can be undone unless good, reliable and dependable care is provided for the children during the parents' absence.

There can be little doubt that parental divorce or separation does create difficulties for children. A large-scale follow-up of over 5,300 children born in 1946 was written up by Michael Wadsworth in 1979. It established that broken homes were related to delinquency; the younger the age of the children at the time of separation, the more serious the effects upon them. Interestingly, it showed that delinquent girls, although few in number, were particularly likely to have been adversely affected by parental separations. It appears that the disagreements preceding the separation, the tendency for children to blame themselves for the break-up, their sense of being rejected, all account for some unhappy experiences for the children which may—although not always—be expressed in poor school performance, anti-social behaviour and delinquency.

Divorce has increased seven-fold in the last thirty years. For a time it was fashionable to claim that it was better for parents to split rather than expose their children to marital disharmony. However, recent research at Exeter University reveals that children whose parents feuded but made the effort to stay together fare better than those whose parents separate (Cockett and Tripp's research, cited in *The Guardian*, 8 February 1994). There is much to be said for parents trying to stay together and to avoid divorce, for children do benefit from having the presence of two parents and of not having to resolve the trauma and dilemmas of separation and divorce. None the less, a qualification must be added. At times separation and divorce is necessary in order to protect wives and children.

I recall standing at my doorway refusing entry to a violent husband: cowering upstairs were his wife and children, all of them bruised from his blows. The daughter of eleven frequently bed-wetted; the son of ten was silent and fearful in the presence of his father; the wife, wanting to make the marriage survive, had stuck it for years until she could take no more. Now her husband shouted at me that he had a right to see his family, while I replied that he had no right to treat them as he did. He smashed his fist repeatedly into the door until his knuckles bled, then turned and stormed off. Shaken—for I was scared—I closed the door and fully approved when the woman took out an injunction against her husband and later divorced him. The divorce was not really of her making. Of course, divorces are to be avoided if possible but when they do come it is worth noting that it is usually the mothers who accept responsibility for the children. They do so knowing that they may well face financial hardship and all the disadvantages of being a lone parent. They deserve some credit for their commitment to their children.

Divorced parents often join with the widowed, the separated and the unmarried to form a collectivity known as single parents. Single parents, and particularly unmarried mothers, have become the target of attack by public figures with much of the blame for delinquency being heaped upon them. The attackers include both socialists, such as the academic Norman Dennis, and right-wing gurus, such as the American Charles Murray. Their argument is that welfare benefits now give young working-class women the economic resources to raise children outside marriage. These young mothers, they continue, often lack parenting skills and, without the support of a father, produce undisciplined children who are unfitted for society, with many turning to crime. Murray even paints a picture of Britain's inner cities and council estates as overrun by what he calls the 'new rabble' of immoral young women who breed with the unemployed, the criminal, the drug abusers, to form a dangerous underclass which is threatening the whole of British civilization.

The number of single parents has increased sharply. Not only amongst the working class, it should be added, but also amongst the wealthy and the aristocracy—although they are given much less attention from people like Charles Murray. The trend is regrettable but it is not of the apocalyptic proportions claimed by the likes of Murray. Single parents make up 19 per cent of all families so that the majority of children, including those in areas of social deprivation, are still brought up by two parents. Further, the effect of single parenthood on children is far more complicated than the critics imply.

Yes, the children of such families are more likely to become delinquent than those from two-parent families. None the less, the majority of children of single parents do not become criminals. The simple equation, *unmarried parenthood = delinquent children* simply does not hold. One study, cited by Utting, showed that amongst young, single mothers who had been brought up in public care—a group associated with having difficulties in coping with children—a significant number did, against all the odds, display good parenting skills. In short, some of the single mothers, trained and encouraged by social workers and given adequate financial support, did become loving and capable parents. This is not to say that single parenthood is desirable; it is to say that it is not an inevitable route to delinquent offspring.

Despite the above qualifications, it must be agreed that children are more likely to avoid delinquency if they are raised by two parents. The reason is that two committed parents can share child care, can lessen the pressures, can bring more involvement and stimulation than one parent. The result is that they have more chance of avoiding the inadequate child-rearing methods which have a negative impact on children's emotional and social growth. The task facing single parents, however, is only made harder if public condemnation and punishing policies are hurled at them. Far better, in my opinion, if the single parents (mostly mothers) who loyally stick with their children are given material and emotional support in bringing up their families.

Neither inevitable nor irreversible

Professor Richard Whitfield, emeritus professor of education at Aston University, writing in *Community Care*, said,

For children to stand the best chance of thriving in our culture, they need, ideally, to experience the unconditional love of a mother and a father figure who are committed both to the child and to each other.

After many years in welfare work I must agree with the tenor of this statement. The research studies show that delinquency does frequently stem from family mal-functioning and that families which separate or split are particularly vulnerable. However, a couple of riders must be added.

First, nothing is inevitable. Some stable marriages do produce delinquent offspring while some lone parents do not. Again, it is generally accepted that children brought up in residential establishments are at greater risk of delinquency. Yet there are exceptions, and some children benefit greatly from their residential experiences.

I have had a long association with Mill Grove which has grown out of the children's home pioneered by the remarkable Herbert White. White, moved by the plight of deprived children, started a small children's home in Woodford, Essex in 1899. It grew rapidly to over eighty children, yet White never appealed for funds and relied for support solely on prayer to God. After the Second World War, the leadership was taken over by Herbert's son and then his grandson, and still continues today. Having researched the record of the home (and met a number of former residents), I know that delinquency has not been a feature of their lives. Today, the homely and loving atmosphere still has the same positive effect on its present youngsters. Nothing is inevitable.

Second, nothing is irreversible. John Bowlby's important research on the adverse effects on children of a lack of affectionate mothering has been followed by other studies which demonstrate that subsequent experiences of caring from loving individuals can modify if not overcome the earlier setbacks. Again, divorce may be devastating for the children but the continuing presence of one loving parent, regular and positive contact with the absent partner and, perhaps, an understanding and warm relationship with a step-parent can ease matters. Human beings are not mechanistic objects who can only act in expected and pre-determined ways. Families can survive emotional and social disadvantages.

Positive families

In identifying the origins of delinquency in family malfunctioning, this book has given a number of somewhat sombre examples of family life. It should be made clear that most families do cope with their children, most of whom do not become habitual criminals. The

Cambridge researcher Kate Painter studied 307 teenage youths on two Midland estates, and found that the majority had good relationships with their parents, that they felt that their parents did spend time with them, and that only a small number admitted to committing serious crimes. Therefore it is timely to end the chapter with a couple of examples of families who do cope, and then to identify their strengths.

Dave and Donna have three children aged seven, five and one. Donna puts the well-being of the children before anything else. She is very concerned about their health and safety. She exudes love yet firmly lays down the ground rules about behaviour such as what to do at mealtimes, how the children treat each other, and how they play with other children. Donna has taken them to a mothers and toddlers group, where she helps, and carefully selects useful toys and books.

Dave works for a national voluntary society in a role which entails much travelling. Despite his business, he carefully puts aside time both to support his wife and to be with the children. He regularly plays with them, reads to them, tells them stories, romps around, and gives them many cuddles and tokens of affection.

These parents are fortunate enough to have a suf-ficient, although not excessive, income. Thus they are able to provide a comfortable environment for a loving yet disciplined family life. I know because my wife and I often stay with them and they come to us. The three children are lively and stimulating and already know how to enjoy and be enjoyed.

The other example concerns an Asian family, written up by Madeleine Bunting in the *Guardian* of 17 September 1991:

Dippy and Rajinder are second-generation Asians and their description of their relationship with their parents offers a striking contrast [to other young people in the article]. *'When I was in my teens, my mother and I were not friends,' says*

Dippy. 'She was very supportive and she was always there. But we didn't talk about a lot of things.'

Her brother, Rajinder, adds: 'I was shocked by the way white friends talked to their parents. It wasn't so much rude but chummy, like they're talking to a friend.'

Dippy and Rajinder treated their parents with respect and a certain formality. The clear distinction between their parents' rules and what the children were allowed to do, Dippy says, contrasted sharply with the confusion she found in the families of her English friends. But authority as they describe it does not fit English preconceptions. 'Asian parents aren't strict about bedtimes or meals,' Rajinder explains. 'Asian kids often stay up until 10 or 11 and run around until they drop. My parents were strict about how I behaved and how the neighbours perceived me. The strictness was related to not giving the family a bad name in the community.'

Both Dippy and Rajinder are now highly successful professionals. They attribute that success to their parents. They admire the enormous changes their parents as immigrants had to make, and praise their flexible but firm attitude.

'Without my parents I wouldn't have got anywhere. I went to the kind of school where most of the kids left to become Heathrow baggage handlers with a couple of CSEs,' says Rajinder, who went to university. 'A lot of kids used to bunk school, but I was petrified of my parents finding out. My mother used to say that if she heard of any trouble she'd be on the teacher's side. That's a very Indian attitude.'

'The youth club used to finish at 10 o'clock and I had to be home by 11 or my parents would have come down on me like a ton of bricks, but my friend, a black guy, could stay out as long as he liked. He got into trouble doing burglaries.'

The authority Dippy and Rajinder describe did not depend on severe punishments. Dippy believes that the 'Asian value of respecting your parents all your life' is the precondition for a non-punitive authority. Now in her mid-thirties, Dippy still says that 'There's no question, not now, not ever, of fighting with my mother. If she says something is to be done, that's the end of it.'

These snapshots of two families, one focussed on young children, the other on grown-up children, reflect the family life of many where the youngsters will probably steer clear of crime. They represent different cultural backgrounds yet their child-rearing methods have certain similarities which appear crucial in the raising of children. These parents

- had the ability to convey affection so that the children felt loved, secure and respected;

- applied firm yet kind discipline so that the children grew to know what was right and wrong, to know what kind of behaviour and attitudes were and were not acceptable;

- concerned themselves with the children's educational and leisure activities where they acquired the educational and social skills to cope satisfactorily in society;

- set models of inter-personal behaviour. That is, the parents displayed positive relationships towards each other and thereby taught the children how to relate, how to settle differences without violence, how to enjoy each other's company.

Children raised in families with the above positive features are likely to find satisfaction in their self-images, in the relationships they make, in their achievements in society. In short, they will not need the status and gains which others seek in crime. When tempted to do delinquent acts, they will know what is right and wrong and will possess the example of their parents and their own values to keep them from succumbing. Delinquent children often seem to lack these advantages and strengths. The second part of this book will concentrate on how they can find them or find compensation for them.

40

THREE

Not Just the Family

Delinquency is moulded by a multitude of factors both inside and outside the family as can be seen in the following two cases.

Lorraine's birth was a difficult one, a forceps delivery. Her parents already had five children so they decided she was the last. The family lived on the estate where I worked as a youth and neighbourhood worker. Dad was a gardener with the council and Mum eventually took a part-time job with the local video shop. I always got on well with the parents and admired the way they had brought up a large family on a limited income.

When she was twelve, Lorraine joined our youth club. She was attractive, active and attention-seeking. And before long she did get the attention of male admirers, but could easily repel them with her outbursts of temper. Aged fourteen, she twice brought the club to an abrupt close when she attacked girls whom she regarded as rivals. When she was sixteen, her parents discovered she was having sex with a boy-friend. When they confronted her, Lorraine retorted, 'Oh, everyone does it,' and stormed out.

Lorraine's attendance at the youth club tailed off as she spent much of her time hanging about the streets, riding on the back of motor bikes and watching videos in friends' houses. Her parents disliked her new mates whom they regarded as 'a bad lot' and told her she should not be watching certain videos—which had been hired from the shop where her mum worked.

Aged seventeen, Lorraine had a job in a petrol service station. She was dismissed for fiddling payments. She turned to me to ask me to get her back pay and to speak for her in court, where she was fined. Her parents were horrified but Lorraine promptly pointed out that her dad had for years brought home plants and tools from work. 'That's different,' spluttered Dad. 'Everybody does it, even the manager, it's a perk.' A great row ensued which culminated with Lorraine rushing out and declaring that she would never return. At midnight, she turned up at our door.

A year later, Lorraine was involved in a number of brawls with girls who had been chatting up her boyfriend. One girl was seriously injured and Lorraine was remanded in custody and later placed on probation. Perhaps the fact that she was pregnant saved her from a custodial sentence. Lorraine's parents wanted her to marry but she refused and set herself up as a one-parent family. To our surprise, she coped pretty well in the first few months of parenthood.

The second case is taken from an article by Madeleine Bunting, printed in the *Guardian* on 17 September 1991.

Chris lives in a tower block. He is a single father bringing up his two-year-old daughter, Lisa. He describes the pressure of a materialistic consumer culture on parents. 'It makes parents feel bad when you can't buy toys for their children. Kids go through fads with clothing and toys and parents feel guilty if they can't give the kids the same as other kids have. Kids are so spiteful to other kids who don't have the right clothes.'

It is a matter of great pride to Chris that 'if Lisa needs something she will get it. She's got a Wendy House, a slide and boxes and boxes of toys. I'll go without to provide for her.'

But one thing Chris cannot give Lisa is a garden, and he feels it keenly. 'I'd love a garden for Lisa but I can't let her out of the flat. The parks are covered in dog shit, so the only place for kids to play is on the deck walkways where the dogs have urinated. On the stairways you see silver paper everywhere —it's been chased for skeg [heroin]. *It's not the right place to bring up a child. It's a hard area: one of the first things your kid learns to do is to fight. Children on this estate can't be children because they are too restricted. I'm always telling Lisa not to do something—either because it's dangerous or because neighbours will complain about the noise.'*

Such an environment makes the task of being a good parent immeasurably harder. It makes the diatribes on the collapse of the family and the decline in parental authority seem irrelevant. We are not up against errant individuals but a materialistic, individualistic culture which has undermined the value we place on the child.

Family life, the ways parents treat their children and the manner in which children respond, do play a major part in determining whether or not the latter do or do not become delinquents. But the ways families perform do not just spring from themselves. The examples of Lorraine, who did turn to crime, and of Chris, who is struggling to ensure that his daughter will not, show that the behaviour of parents, children and young people is also subject to forces over which they have little control. Consider some of these forces:

Birth complications

Lorraine was a forceps delivery. Professor Adrian Raine, a former prison psychologist, has completed large-scale studies of criminals. He found that children who suffered birth trauma or were rejected by their parents within a year did not become more violent than average. But those who suffered both birth difficulties and rejection were particularly likely to later commit violent crime. Indeed, the 4 per cent who experienced both were responsible for 22 per cent of subsequent crimes by his research samples.

The reasons are not certain but the professor suggests that some form of brain damage caused at birth was reinforced by rejection which then found outlets in violence. Readers whose own children have suffered traumatic births should not panic. Our own daughter had a forceps delivery. She has not turned out a violent criminal, although she has become a gynaecologist!

Family size

Lorraine was a member of a large family. The research by West and Farrington cited in *The Delinquent Way of Life* confirms other studies that children from large families are somewhat more subject to delinquency. Again, parents with many children should not be alarmed. Most such children do not become criminals. The finding is that they are more at risk. It appears that parents with five, six or more children do find it more difficult to give attention to, and to control them. Family structure, not just parenting ability, is an important factor.

Peer groups

As she got older, Lorraine was subject to pressure from friends of her age, sometimes called a peer group. During her teens, these friends seemed to influence her more than her parents. Chris worried about the future pressures on his daughter in an area where children soon picked up that they were expected to fight and where drug-taking was common. Further, he felt that an environment of a tower block militated against efforts to be a good parent. The influence of a depriving environment and of peer groups will be taken up in succeeding chapters.

Public forces

Birth, family structures, peer groups, and social environment all influence family life, and because they are experienced by the family, they are probably understood by them as influences. Less immediate but also powerful are attitudes and values which are commonplace in society. For instance, when criticized for their behaviour both Lorraine and her dad justified it by retorting, 'Everyone does it.' These pressures spring from the media, from public debate, from the examples and communications of important figures and corporate bodies. This chapter will now focus on the forces of the mass media and public morality to see if they have any bearing on delinquency.

The media

Popular means of communication—the media—have often been accused of fostering delinquency. At one time, comics, particularly American ones, were blamed. Soon after the last war, the cinema gained a great hold on the British public. In our family, Mum took the children, along with a packed tea, every Thursday to whatever film was showing. On Saturday we swarmed in with hundreds of other kids to sing 'We come along on Saturday morning, Greeting everybody with a smile', and to cheer Rin Tin Tin and Abbott and Costello. Obviously the cinema was reaching young minds and in 1947 Herbert White was convinced 'that two-thirds of the juvenile crime today is the result of the cinema'. Herbert was a great Christian leader whose biography I have written. But his statement was made without any evidence.

Cinema-going declined, yet film-watching is more widespread than ever, for films are now shown on TV and video-recorders. Television is a most powerful means of modern communication, even more influential than newspapers, simply because it reaches into almost every home. And what is shown is very different from the Ealing comedies which we queued to see. In one average week in 1993, British TV showed 737 dead bodies, 1,117 people injured, and 343 sex scenes. Some of these incidents were on news programmes but most were on feature films, dramas and soaps. The terrestrial channels, BBC1, BBC2, ITV and Channel 4 showed less of them than the satellite channels run by BSkyB and Sky One, but even on the former, 52 per cent of all programmes contained some violence. Gone are the days of *Dixon of Dock Green* when any violence was implicit rather than explicit, when criminals were not cast in a glamorous light, and when the goodies and the baddies were distinct categories.

Does modern TV adversely affect young people? Its critics claim that it feeds a diet of violence and crime to impressionable young minds. Its defenders retort that viewers can enjoy TV without copying it.

Television is also under fire for the manner it deals with matters of sexual morality. The numerous soaps revolve around sexual relationships. Sex becomes predominant, with the danger that it stimulates the sex crimes of abuse, assault and rape. Another danger is that popular TV programmes can give the impression that moving in together, separating, divorce, changing partners, re-marrying and so on are all easy steps. They convey little of the long-lasting pain they inflict upon individuals, the harm done to children and the weakening of virtues like fidelity. If television does contribute to the easy accep-tance of such behaviour then it does us a disservice for, as was shown, children of broken and re-ordered families often face difficulties which can make them more vulnerable to delinquency.

Of course, it must be added that many TV programmes—particularly documentaries and current affairs programmes such as *Panorama*—can and do deal with social topics in sensible and balanced ways. Having watched more TV during a period of unemployment, I can affirm that many day-time and schools' and children's programmes are of a quality to satisfy even Mary Whitehouse. Television can be a medium for good or evil. It follows that programmes could stimulate attitudes and actions which either promote or prevent delinquency. The major question is, which way will the pendulum swing? Unfortunately, the signs are that all forms of television will be increasingly dominated by commercial interests and hence the content of sex and violence may increase rather than decrease.

More worrying than even the course of TV is the particular effects of horror films shown mainly on satellite TV or hired from local shops to show on home video machines, now in 70 per cent of homes. The films, known as video nasties, contain scenes of sadism, cruelty, abuse, rape and murder. The issue, a longstanding one, re-emerged in the James Bulger case when the judge criticized a film—*Child's Play 3*, which had been viewed by an estimated 181,000 children on satellite TV and was readily available in video shops. Apparently it was seen by the guilty boys and it showed similarities with the ways in which they attacked James Bulger. Previously, the same film had been referred to in another murder trial in which one of six killers chanted a line from it as the victim was tortured.

For years, the prevailing wisdom—which has suited the commercial interests in the entertainment industry—has been that violent images do not influence child behaviour. The debunking view is at odds with two everyday factors: one is that television clearly does influence behaviour, otherwise companies would not spend millions of pounds on TV advertising; the other is that youth workers, teachers and others who have close contact with a range of children do observe them excitedly discussing the video nasties, re-enacting them in play, and sometimes repeating them in real and violent behaviour against other children. To them, it came as no surprise when Professor Elizabeth Newson published a report in 1994, *Video Violence and the Protection of Children*, signed by twenty-five leading psychologists and psychiatrists, which confirmed a link between the videos and abnormal behaviour. One result of the report was an announcement by the Home Office that the British Board of Film Classification would be given greater powers to classify, cut, or even ban, such videos.

No doubt, video nasties on TV and video machines will continue. Such films do not influence all children in the same way. The evidence suggests that violent programmes have most effect on children who already have aggressive predispositions. Thus a large number of children may watch films such as *The Exorcist* or *Taxi Driver,* and most will not have their actions directly affected. But a minority may well have their violent tendencies reinforced to the point in which their subsequent hostility copies the criminal methods they have seen. Further, and more widespread in effect, other research suggests that continual exposure to violence on the screens makes it more acceptable. The academics call this 'desensitization'. The outcome is that a few children behave more aggressively in a society in which violent crime is taken less seriously.

Public messages

The views and ethics of public figures and powerful corporations, as well as the examples they set, are now more widely known and therefore more influential than they were even twenty years ago, simply because of the outreach of television and, to a lesser extent, radio and newspapers, which have expanded rapidly since the 1940s. In what ways do they touch family life and delinquency?

Government in Britain, both national and local, has always claimed to uphold law and order, to defend honesty, family life and moral uprightness. Occasionally, scandals did surface when the actions of politicians appeared to be in conflict with the standards they professed. Thus in 1922, the Prime Minister Lloyd George's 'sale of honours' in return for party political donations was considered dishonourable. Significantly, Lloyd George's sexual adventures were not made public even by journalists who knew about them.

It is difficult to say whether the sexual standards of public figures have declined. What is certain is that their misdeeds are much more publicized, as the popular press spends hundreds of thousands of pounds to splash their stories across the front pages. And the editors of such papers are sometimes rewarded by the politicians with knighthoods! Of the drop in honesty and integrity, however, there can be little doubt.

In January 1994, the Commons Public Accounts Committee issued a devastating report on mismanagement, incompetence and fraud in public bodies, especially quangos. The complaints ranged from individuals utilizing cheap or free housing for themselves and relatives, to massive overpayments for pensions, to a regional health authority wasting £20 million on a computer system. It concluded that the old public standards of impartiality, objectivity and honesty were under threat. The Committee would have done well to turn its gaze into its own House of Commons.

It is not unknown for a government minister to guide privatization legislation through Parliament and later to be rewarded with a seat on the board of the private company concerned. Such action is not illegal, but it does entail the minister using his post for subsequent private gain. Another minister—a prominent church-goer—received £17,000 from public funds for security improvements to his home which the police said were unnecessary, while he also failed to declare that a private company had spent £2,000 to restore a pond in the garden where he received visitors. In 1994 it was revealed that an MP had been appointed as a parliamentary secretary to the Treasury although he had headed a firm which had gone bankrupt. Moreover, a government body had written off a substantial loan to that company. No action was taken against the MP. And the list could go on. Public concern did push the government into establishing a committee under Lord Nolan. Its report *Standards in Public Life* was published in 1995 and its recommendations are under consideration.

It is not just one political party. All-party support was given to legislation to give ministers substantial pay-offs when they left office. Accordingly, one took £12,639 when he left to become Governor of Bermuda, another £5,000 —which must have seemed like chicken-feed against his personal fortune of £40 million—and a former Chancellor of the Exchequer received £8,000 to add to an additional £50,000 a year for jobs in the City, while continuing to draw his MP's salary and considerable expenses. These actions and perks have given rise to a new term—sleaze.

The decline in public standards and the rise of sleaze may well be linked with the prevailing economic philosophy of the last fifteen years. In a reaction to state welfare and expenditure, right-wing politicians, now called the New Right, took on board the doctrines of the American Milton Friedman. His basic premise was that as much human activity as possible should be left to private enterprise in a free market.

'Free' implied that the market should suffer few, if any, restrictions from legislation, such as regulations to protect employees, and that any saleable commodity—be it food, arms, old people's homes, health services and now, Friedman adds, even hard drugs—should be bought and sold in order to make a profit. The driving force of the market was seen as human selfishness, which was regarded as a virtue in that it stimulates human enterprise and production. As the then government minister, John Redwood, puts it, 'The public interest is taken care of by the private interest of wanting to make money.' The doctrines of the New Right were taken on board by the Governments of the 1980s and 1990s, thus leading to large-scale privatization of former public utilities, the abolition of laws to protect low wage-earners, the introduction of market practices into health and welfare services, and reductions on the taxes of the most affluent citizens.

To be sure, the policies of the New Right have brought some positive contributions. Their criticisms of bureaucracy within the civil service were justified. Few would deny that industrial and social services require efficient management. The drawback has been the victory of greed, for the uncontrolled free market allows full play to human selfishness with little regard for others. Thus company directors have awarded themselves massive salary increases while cutting the wages of their workers or even sacking them. A huge rise in unemployment and an increase of numbers of those living in poverty from three to eleven million is dismissed as merely the price to be paid for a market system. Of course, there have been dissenting voices, with George Carey, the Archbishop of Canterbury, notable among them, but the overwhelming message from government and business has been that the goal is to make money for oneself.

Perhaps my strictures about public corruption and the promotion of greed are shaped by a bitterness from living in a neighbourhood where over 70 per cent of children come from poor homes, in a country which is one of the richest in the world. So it is as well to add the judgment of an insider, David Alton, an MP with a reputation for integrity, writing in *Third Way* in June 1994. Admitting that there is now 'wide-ranging and insidious corruption in politics and government', he continues,

The motivation behind our sleazy state is as old as the hills; the pursuit of power, personal aggrandisement and the protection of privilege. We have passed through a decade when we were all encouraged to consume and acquire. The 'me first' society in which everything had a price and nothing a value promoted as good business practice unbridled individualism, personal greed and rapacious competitiveness. As government has adopted business practice at the expense of service, so the values of the financial jungle have become the civic values of our own time.

The real tragedy is that most politicians do not regard such a morality as corrupt. Some will even defend it as sound market practice. Meanwhile, the public has come to expect nothing better from the system.

A decline in public morality, the growth of corruption and sleaze within government, the victory of the economics of greed. What has all this to do with juvenile crime? The answer is threefold.

First, it contributes to a lack of respect for authority. Crime is partly held in check when figures of authority—law-makers, law-upholders, teachers, parents, and so on—are held in such respect that what they stand for is not lightly broken. In Britain, a major source of authority has been Parliament and, within it, the Government, which is expected to formulate laws which are just and whose members are expected to uphold both moral and statutory laws. Yet in Britain a national poll published by *The Observer* in 1993 found that, in rating institutions which could be trusted, the public put the Government bottom and Parliament next to bottom. If public figures, particularly law-makers, are held to be untrustworthy, then the laws themselves and the keeping of laws are undermined. It follows that the very concept of benign authority throughout society is weakened. In 1992, the Prime Minister blamed delinquency on the fact that 'many no longer drew a distinction between right and wrong.' His assertion is probably correct but he failed to add that many public figures had failed to make that distinction in their political and business lives. It was thus hardly surprising if others, lower down the social scale, followed suit.

Second, the Government's stated belief in the value of family life is seen as being at odds with the practice of its members. If cabinet ministers and other prominent figures change partners, have children out of wedlock, divorce, re-marry, and so on, then they sanction such practices throughout society. Lorraine's response to her parents was, 'Oh, everyone does it.' Soon after she was a single mother. The Government often bewails the extent of juvenile crime yet often its members do not encourage the stability and permanency of family life which is a bulwark against its growth.

Third, the obsession with personal, material gain, sometimes accompanied by sleaze or corruption, now permeates society. Lorraine's dad justified his fiddling with, 'Everybody does it, even the manager. It's a perk.' He had not foreseen the effect on his daughter. Many young people are now reared in a culture where newspaper articles, TV advertisements and economic philosophies all stress the desirability of accumulating consumer goods and in which public figures give the message, 'Grab all you can.'

Faced with the pressures to accumulate, along with a greater acceptance of sleaze, it is hardly surprising if youngsters, unable to find gratification in legal ways, do so by illegal ones. Professor of criminology Robert Reiner explains that 'The crime explosion corresponds closely to the adoption of free-market economic strategies (not only here but in many other countries, most evidently Eastern Europe, which has also experienced a massive rise in crime).' This is not a condemnation of the free market system as such but rather a regret that it has become a vehicle for putting selfishness at the top of the personal shopping list. For this public figures and public bodies must take some blame.

Lorraine's delinquency cannot be understood without reference to her background, her neighbourhood, her friends, her work. Chris's struggle to keep his daughter away from delinquent pressures cannot be appreciated without knowledge of the tower block in which he lives and the materialistic culture persuading him to spend more and more. The delinquency of others cannot be explained without taking into account the effect on them of the values, practices and examples of the mass media and public leaders. Yet this is not to let either the delinquents or their parents completely off the hook. Individuals are not puppets; they have the responsibility to react to, deal with, and challenge those outside forces. Delinquency must be viewed through binoculars which can focus both on the immediate individuals and also on the distant environment. A similar focus will be required when considering the effects of poverty.

FOUR

The Crime of Poverty

Fifteen-year-old Bert stood at my door. He had been expelled from school five months ago and still a new school could not be found which would accept him. 'Mum wants to see you, Bob.'

I gave Bert a biscuit and pocketed an orange for his youngest brother before we made our way the few hundred yards to the block of flats where they lived. Mum was in a mood.

'I can't get him to clean his room,' she complained, 'Can't you tell him, Bob?' Mrs B. was a widow left with debts and five children. She found it difficult to control Bert and sometimes asked me to act as a kind of father- or grandfather-figure. We went up to his room. It contained two beds and some scraps of carpet. Patches of damp blackened the ceiling and walls. There were no cupboards for clothes and toys. No wonder that Bert and his brother found it difficult to keep tidy. Back with his mum, I suggested we look for some secondhand cupboards. Mum agreed. Released, Bert went out.

I talked with Mrs B. She received £97.40 a week Income Support for herself and four children. An older son, Pat, who also lived there had been in prison for burglary. He was heavily into drugs and, when his money ran out, would demand from his mum. 'I can't cope, I can't go on,' she sometimes sobbed. But she always did.

As I left, Bert and his young brother ran over and asked if I would take them swimming. I agreed, adding my usual silly proviso, 'If you're good.' They rarely left the estate and to go for a ride in the minibus to the Leisure Pool was a great treat for them. As I climbed into the vehicle, I looked around and saw a flat where I'd helped a drug abuser who had been stabbed. Most people in the street were unemployed. I thought to myself, 'What chance has Bert got? He's in the midst of poverty and deprivation. He'll go the same way. He'll end up a criminal like Pat.'

Poverty is extensive in Britain, whichever of the three main measures are used:

- The Benefits Poverty Level counts as poor all those dependent upon incomes at or below the basic level of Income Support. By this measure in 1989, some 11.3 million people were poor.

- The Income Poverty Level regards as poor all those with incomes less than 50 per cent of average income. In 1990–91, 13.5 million citizens, 24 per cent of the population, were in this plight.

- The Basic Essentials Level stems from the Breadline Britain survey conducted by London Weekend TV. It asked members of the public which items they considered as essential necessities and they chose items like a damp-free home, an inside toilet, a waterproof coat, an annual holiday, heating for living areas and so on. People without three or more items were then graded as poor. The total for Britain was 11 million people.

Given the amount of poverty, it is hardly surprising that crime rates are so high. Or is it? Just around the corner from Bert's is another family I know well. They too are poor, yet so far the children have not become delinquent.

The contrast between these two families reflects a debate in Britain. Some see a definite connection between poverty and crime. Others deny it and in November 1993 the Home Secretary, Michael Howard, poured scorn on 'trendy theories' which attributed delinquency to socio-economic factors. Yet, soon after, Joe Whitty, the head of a young offenders' institution which comes under the Home Office, stated in the press, 'Policy-makers might refuse to acknowledge it, but youths in the criminal justice system are poor, disadvantaged and socially and educationally inept.' Again, in May 1994 the Police Federation in a lively debate defeated the motion that 'crime is inevitably linked to deprivation.' Yet many supported the claim and Sir John Smith, president of the Association of Chief Police Officers, later stated that unemployment and a lack of facilities were creating a cycle of criminality.

Crime is widespread

Crime is certainly not restricted to people with low incomes. Fraud within the City of London has escalated in recent years. Tax evasion is massive. In 1991–92, the Inland Revenue recovered £5 billion as a result of its investigations, although this is considered to be just a fraction of the real amount lost. Crime is widespread.

Similarly, crime is found amongst all kinds of youngsters. The Centre for Criminology at the University of Edinburgh interviewed a cross-section of eleven- to fifteen-year-olds and found that 69 per cent said that they had committed an offence within the previous nine months. The fact that some middle-class children become delinquent is no surprise for, as described in an earlier chapter, even the most wealthy parents can deprive their offspring of love and attention. However, in regard to the Edinburgh survey, it should be noted that the figures depend on self-reporting—that is, whether children say they broke the law, not on whether they were caught and prosecuted. Even among the reported offences, the majority were of a very minor nature. Only 3 per cent admitted to house-breaking. The evidence suggests that the most serious crimes and the most persistent offenders are found amongst youngsters from low-income backgrounds. There *is* some overlap between crime and poverty.

The overlap

Large-scale studies are agreed that delinquents have a tendency to come from low-income and socially deprived families. The survey *Continuities of Deprivation*, headed by Kolvin, established that six out of ten boys from such backgrounds acquired a criminal record. Another survey, by West and Farrington, *The Delinquent Way of Life*, noted that offenders were most likely to have parents who were poor and who resided in areas of run-down housing. As David Utting concluded after reviewing the relevant research, 'Children whose families suffer financial and environmental poverty are clearly at greater risk than those whose parents have the income to provide them with a comfortable, uncrowded home.' Again, in 1995, the National Association for the Care and Rehabilitation of Offenders published a study by eighteen experts, including a chief police officer, and chaired by Professor David Donnison. It concluded that crime was closely associated with inequality and poverty.

Given the connection with poverty, it is to be expected that offenders tend to be concentrated in geographical districts of social deprivation. During 1993–94, a number of youth 'riots' occurred in Britain when gangs of young people threw stones at the police, vandalized buildings, started fires, and stole cars. These illegal actions did not flare up in Tunbridge Wells or Cheltenham Spa. Characteristically, they broke out in inner cities and council estates where life is bleakest.

The estate where I live consists of 90 per cent council housing. The local authority housing department is refurbishing many properties and improving the environment.

Yet much of the area has the appearance of decay with many of the tenement flats suffering from damp and one in four of them empty and boarded up. In 1991 its few square miles suffered 5,384 crimes of housebreaking, 2,567 assaults, and 1,538 acts of vandalism. In all, the area suffered 260 recorded crimes per week—a rate double that of more prosperous suburbs nearby. Noticeably, within the area, drug-related offences have risen steeply as dealers target socially-deprived zones.

The overlap between crime and poverty is also revealed in the kinds of groups with high incidences of crime. For instance, homeless young people are probably the poorest members of society. Often they have no money at all and no permanent roof over their heads. They are tempted to commit offences to obtain food and clothes, and are also a prey for those wanting to lure them into prostitution and the drug culture. A report by the housing charity Shelter found that 37 per cent of young homeless people had been in trouble with police within the previous twelve months.

The unemployed are another low-income group. Unemployment has risen dramatically since 1979, reaching almost three million at times. The young have been particularly hard hit so that in 1993 over 23 per cent of sixteen- to nineteen-year-olds and 17 per cent of twenty- to twenty-four-year-olds were out of work. Probation officers began to observe that many of their clients were unemployed. In 1992, in Manchester, 85 per cent of those dealt with by the probation service were without jobs. The trend was confirmed a year later in a survey by senior probation officers which found that nationally 70 per cent of serious offences were committed by the unemployed.

Subsequent research has charted the rise of burglaries against that of unemployment. The Cambridge economist David Dickinson studied the connection using a sample of unemployed males aged seventeen to twenty-five. He found that the number of burglaries dropped during mini-booms but rose during periods of recession when jobs were lost.

However, the relationship between poverty and crime is not straightforward. Figures from the Home Office show that certain crimes, such as sex offences and assault, actually rise with increased prosperity—a rise blamed on higher levels of alcohol consumption. The same figures also show that it is property crime, such as theft, burglary and car-stealing, which escalates during periods of greater unemployment and poverty.

It is not being argued that all poor people become criminals. Far from it, for the majority do not. Rather, the evidence is that children and young people who come from low-income homes, who live in deprived areas, who are unemployed, are *at greater risk* of committing offences. The next question is why? Why is poverty linked with crime?

The advantages of affluence

One reason why poor people feature more prominently in crime statistics is that their affluent counterparts are less likely to be investigated, apprehended or prosecuted. Inner-city areas and council estates tend to have a higher concentration of police and other officials. Residential suburbs are less regulated and hence wrong-doers are less visible. Again, problematic but privileged children have options which can steer them away from public intervention. For instance, in 1994 a government minister's son was expelled from boarding school for 'school-disrupting reasons'. The police did not prosecute. The boy's behaviour did not bring him under the scrutiny of local authority case reviews. Instead, other acceptable and expensive care was found for him. By contrast, disruptive pupils in state schools can be expelled and left for months without alternative schooling and, in Scotland, may be referred to the Reporter who can summon them to a Children's Hearing.

Finally, there is evidence that, even if prosecuted and convicted, the affluent receive lighter sentences. In the City of London, whizz-kids who embezzle hundreds of thousands of pounds tend to receive fines or other non-custodial sentences. Young shoplifters from housing estates are in danger of prison sentences. Criminal but privileged young people may well be represented in court by top lawyers who, backed by articulate parents, can impress the judges or magistrates. In a study of institutions for young offenders, Cairine Petrie found not one inmate whose parents were rich or in professional occupations. The scales of justice tend to be weighed against the poverty-stricken.

The disadvantages of unemployment

Unemployed people are vulnerable to crime. The economic journalist, Will Hutton, writes, 'Unemployment is the single most important cause of poverty and plays a key role in provoking family breakdown, social distress and the growth of criminality.' The unemployed tend to be poor and the combination of poverty and unemployment is associated with crime for three main reasons.

First, unemployed young people can become so desperate that they steal to survive. A young father shop-lifts to feed his baby. A single mother came to me and tearfully admitted that she had stolen a purse from another shopper's bag: she was fined £180 and, unable to pay, was fearful that she would be imprisoned and her children removed into public care. A long-term un-employed father returned to find his flat wrecked and his TV stolen: unable to afford a new one, he stole from someone else to replace it.

Stealing for essentials is not new. The Christian politician George Lansbury observed it in the East End of London in the 1930s. He wrote of unemployed 'young lads between sixteen and twenty-one years of age' who left home to avoid becoming a 'burden to their parents and friends. Many of these young men take to petty crime. Some become inured to crime and turn into criminals on a large scale.' Yet, as Lansbury asked, in moral terms are they any more criminal than the powerful figures who cause and tolerate unemployment? The sobering fact is that today more young people are out of work than in Lansbury's time. They are also submitted to a barrage of media advertising exhorting them to possess more consumer goods. Some steal. As it says in the biblical book of Proverbs (chapter 30, verse 9), 'If a man is rich he may think he has no need of God, but if he is poor he may steal.'

Second, unemployment can entail a sense of boredom and futility that sometimes leads to delinquency. Jobless youngsters may not only be poor; they may be confined to isolated estates like Hartcliffe in Bristol, Blackbird Leys in Oxford and Ely in Cardiff. They can rarely afford to travel into, let alone enjoy, the leisure facilities in city centres. For some, excitement and status is therefore sought in throwing firebombs, abusing the police, running around in gangs, or stealing cars. This does not excuse their behaviour but it does explain it.

Even the excitement of mini-riots can wane. Perhaps more seriously, long-term unemployed young people, seeing no future and no hope, may turn to taking drugs such as cannabis, cocaine, temazepam and heroin. Obviously drugs have a chemical effect which induce a buzz or heightened impressions or other 'feel good' experiences. Not so generally recognized is that drug-taking also provides access into a social network of other abusers. It is a network which provides friendship, company, a sense of belonging. In it, the users can share their experiences: how they travelled to London, could not find work or housing and then returned to their estate where at least they had shelter, how they find relief in drugs, how to use drugs, and how to find money to pay for them. The last point is significant, for drugs are not cheap, yet, once hooked, the users must pay. 'Eggs', as temazepam tablets are called, may be £1.50 each, while heroin addicts may require up to £200 a day. To generate that kind of money, the young people have to resort to stealing or drug-dealing themselves. Nonetheless, the drug-users are mostly small-time criminals who shoplift, housebreak and purse-snatch. Their addictions are fed by drug barons who import and distribute drugs and fight amongst themselves. Strathclyde police estimate that in Glasgow drug deals are worth around £180 million a year, with trade concentrated on the outlying council estates.

It should not be implied that drug-taking is restricted to unemployed people and deprived areas. After all, some students are known to take them and cocaine is said to be snorted amongst young business executives. But dealers do home in on unemployed young people who appear to have little to do in locations of urban deprivation. And it appears to be increasing.

Third, unemployment may well adversely affect the roles of fathers. Ours is a society which tends to value men according to their jobs or occupations. Unemployed men can feel excluded and devalued. Certainly, some cope, but others appear to react by establishing their masculinity by macho behaviour. They attempt to control their partners and children by force. Angela Phillips, in her controversial book *The Trouble With Boys*, claims that their sons then model themselves on violence which, in turn, can lead to crime. It seems that unemployment can negatively shape family life. And so can poverty in general.

Poverty and parenting

Parenting is hard work in the best of circumstances. For parents on low incomes, even well-intentioned parents who want the very best for their children, the task is made more difficult both in the short term and also in the long term. Sometimes poverty leads to a crisis which then upsets the upbringing of the children.

A single parent I knew was offered cash by a loan shark just before Christmas. 'Here you are, hen, take it, give the kids something nice on Christmas Day.' She took the money. The children enjoyed the presents. Then by January she was due to pay back £45 a week, with the total increasing each time she failed to pay. The shark's thugs banged on her door while the tearful children cowered inside. Then they smashed all the windows of the flat with the threat that she would be next to be smashed unless she paid. The petrified mother gathered her children, borrowed the coach fares, and fled to another town, where they finished up in a Homeless Families Unit. I lost touch but I know the children had been subjected to fear, violence and insecurity which may well have harmed their development.

Crises brought about by lack of money can lead to family conflict. One family kept an alsatian dog for protection. One day it broke a leg in the street and one son, with some presence of mind, nipped into a call box and summoned a vet. Fine. The vet came promptly, removed and treated the dog. But the fee was £50 and the family could not pay, for £50 was half their weekly income. The smaller children kept badgering the mother and the teenage youngsters to get back their beloved dog. One of the teenagers suggested that they saved the £50 by cutting down on food but the mother angrily objected that it was impossible to reduce their food budget by any more. Tempers flared. Meanwhile, every day the dog remained with the vet he charged extra boarding fees. Then he threatened legal action to get his money. The children blamed the mother for not having enough money, the mother blamed the son for calling a private vet instead of the PDSA: a family uproar brought about by £50—or lack of it.

Eventually the family asked me to help, and I negoti-ated with the vet to get him to halve his fee and then took the dog to the PDSA. This incident is almost a farce, yet it has a serious side, for it exposed the children to family arguments and conflict. The experience is not unusual. Shortage of money does bring worries, tensions and disputes.

A study by Professor Jonathan Bradshaw and Hilary Holmes of families living long-term on welfare benefits found that 59 per cent admitted to strong disagreements over money. Rudolph Schaffer, professor of psychology at the University of Strathclyde, concludes that family conflict is almost always damaging to children. He writes, 'There is now overwhelming evidence that conflict produces all sorts of undesirable effects on children, and is probably the single most pernicious cause of maladjustment.' All families, including affluent ones, have some conflicts. But there is little doubt that poverty can lead to crises which increase the likelihood of family arguments. After all, a vet's fee is unlikely to disrupt the lives of most families.

In the long term, poverty means not just a disturbing crisis but also a relentless, grinding struggle to survive. It entails a daily material pressure which is unknown to the majority of people. Consider the lifestyle of two families whom I knew for several years. I asked one woman to keep a diary for a period. She wrote so well that part of it was later published in *The Guardian*, 14 December 1988.

What is it like to try and live on Income Support? Carol Irvine and her family live on the Easterhouse council estate outside Glasgow. This is her story:

Thursday. *The Giro (£61.19) never came till 11 am. Kids never had breakfast. Paid my debts which is £5 to the Provvy for Christmas presents two years ago and £5 to a catalogue for a quilt and a duvet. Then I spent £4.24 on food, £1.21 on tobacco and fag papers and 80p on kids' pants. Total today is £16.25 so I have £44.94 left over.*

Friday. *A letter from school saying they are getting their pictures taken. I just can't afford them. Spent £6.57 on food and left with £38.37.*

Saturday. *Shopping like this: Loaf 45p, milk 52p, two tins meat 90p, 6lb potatoes 50p, pudding 40p, six eggs 45p, marg 20p, soap £1.00, tobacco £1.21. Total for day £5.63, now left with £32.74.*

Sunday. *My birthday today. Clare wanted to give me a card so I gave her 30p. But all the cards were more so she could not buy one. We spent the 30p on sweets. Spent £5.54 of food, so left with £27.20.*

Monday. *Had to go to the chemists. £1.40 on bus fares. Bought plasters, shampoo and toilet rolls at £2.57 and spent £4.47 on food, £1.55 on cleaning materials and £1.21 on tobacco. Total £11.20, left with £16.00.*

Tuesday. *Jim has not got a job. It's not for the lack of wanting. Today his fare to the Job Centre was 70p just for them to tell him there's nothing. That 70p could have been in my kid's pockets. Clare and Doreen had 50p today for the school panto. Doreen ripped her socks at school so that's another pair—and Gordon's—costing £1.38. Spent £6.66 on food today. Went to meeting at Salvation Army and put in 50p. Left with £6.26. Not a lot, is it?*

Wednesday. *Spent £1.00 on light bulbs and £4.44 on food. Now got 82p left so I can get the kids a packet of sweets when the van comes. We just get by.*

Following Monday. *Drew out my month's Child Benefit, £87. I then do my month's main shop. Spent £38.39 on vests, pants and shoes for the children; £1.03 on face cloth, brush and sponge; £2.97 on three toys; £17.00 on new pans (ours was stolen from the window) and tin opener; £15.00 on month's TV rental.*

Then into Glasgow to wash-house. It costs £1.70 to do the washing and £2.80 fares. I was ashamed to bring my laundry out in front of people. The sheets are all torn with being washed and washed. I haven't got one whole sheet. Two of the kids wet the bed so if it wasn't for the rubber mats I'd need a new mattress. Now the mats are torn. Can't buy them with the £2.72 left over.

Jim and I have been together for six years and always been on social security. The last time we went out for a meal together was five years ago on our wedding anniversary. There are things you have to do without. I can't go to a shop for my hair. You can't take the children out.

Most of your money goes on food. But my kids hardly ever have fruit. They have vegetables but it's out of tins. Same with meat, not fresh, always tins. The only shop around here is the van and he's awful expensive. I do go up the market where you get cheap bashed-in tins of stew.

Two of the children get school dinners. There have been times in the holidays when they go without a proper meal but I've always managed to scrape up something even if it's a plate of chips. Sometimes Jim and I go without anything to eat.

The other thing is clothes. When I get the Child Benefit each month I go and buy the clothes for the children but it's all cheap stuff and it never lasts. I bought them shoes, not cheap, £7.99 a pair, but if I could have paid £15 they would last much longer. Even there it's quite expensive. It cost me £7 for two dresses and a cardigan. Otherwise I wait for the jumble sales for my pants, bras, jumpers.

The worst thing about living on Income Support is when you can't get things for the kids. My kids can't get to brush their teeth. I went to buy a tube of toothpaste and they wanted £1.15. Just the other day, my daughter came home from school and said her pal wants her to go to her birthday party. She almost went into a fit when I told her that I could not afford a present. It hurt me too.

If I see a bottle in the street, I'll pick it up and the kids can get the 10p on it at the van and they can have crisps or sweets for school because it's horrible if other kids have got it at playtime and mine haven't.

Sometimes you've got to borrow and that's hard. At times I've not had a slice of bread or a tea bag. Once I went to my brother's and he gave me three hamburgers between the five of us. It was the best the guy could do. Sometimes they borrow off us if I've just stacked up after getting my Giro. Once I had to go to the Social Work Dept. They gave me something but said, 'You'll never get it again.' I'm trying my hardest not to get into debt this Christmas. I think I'll have to but I don't want to go to the money-lenders.

I hate what people say because you're on the Social. Some people think I shouldn't smoke. It's not often that I get a whole packet but it's like Valium, it calms me. You get bother around here. I had to call the police because boys were smashing our windows. If I hadn't had my cigs, I'd have done murder.

It makes me sick that film stars and entertainers get so much money. I had a dream a while back that I was the boss of the world. I made all the film stars get a good wage but hundreds not thousands. And people on income supplement got a good income and those that worked a bit better.

I don't want a lot of money. If I can get my kids their dinner every day and sometimes a pudding and if I can get Jim his half ounce then we are happy in the evening. It's not bad here in Easterhouse. I would like a park for the kids. Near our in-laws there's a park that's got a shute [a slide] and two swings. That's fairyland to my kids.

We all pull together and we get by with the skin of our teeth.

In the case of the second family, I kept the diary, published in *The Guardian*, 12 June 1991:

I see a friend, living on Income Support, almost every day and have compiled a diary of one week in her life. Esther lives with Ernie and their two boys, as well as an older girl by a previous relationship. The DSS stopped her Child Benefit books, adding the amount for the boys on to the Income Support and freezing the other. Esther has protested that she needs the books as Ernie does not give her enough.

Friday: *As on other days, Esther takes and collects her boys from the local authority nursery school and a crèche run by the local Community Association. The Housing Department's 24-hour emergency team arrives, after much pestering, to replace a window smashed by a brick.*

At 1p.m. Esther keeps the appointment at the DSS, some two or three miles away. She has a long wait with her two small children and she hopes Ernie is at home to meet her daughter out of school. The DSS official informs her that the Child Benefit books have been withdrawn because previously she has lost them. He says that payments for the boys will continue to be added to Ernie's Income

Support, while that for her daughter will be paid in lump sums in arrears. Esther alleges that the official rebuked her for writing to her MP about the matter. She returns home at 4.45.

Saturday: *The usual fortnightly giro does not arrive. Phones an emergency number who says it was sent.*

Sunday: *Borrows £15 to buy food. The daughter, washing up, drops their only plates. Goes to Salvation Army for replacements.*

Monday: *Phones DSS, who says giro cannot be replaced until missing one is traced. Goes to Social Work Department but it cannot help. With a friend goes to a solicitor to pursue the Child Benefit matter.*

The nursery school head tells Esther that the promise of special counselling for her son has been arranged for Thursday. Esther is pleased but fearful that her child might be taken from her. Realises that she has no money for the fares to attend the counselling some six miles away. Goes back to the Social Work Department, which is about to shut, and she is told to return next day.

Thursday: *Takes son to counselling, which she finds helpful. Letter from Housing Department says that due to rent arrears it will shortly move to take "recovery of possession" of the flat. Esther alarmed at the threat of eviction and puzzled because she had applied for Housing Benefit.*

Friday: *With a friend, goes to Housing Department, where an official asks why she has not come in response to earlier warning letters. When Esther explains no such letters have come, the official sharply tells her 'to sort that out with the Post Office'. Esther fills in another Housing Benefit form.*

Afternoon, goes to a charity for some second-hand clothes. The health visitor calls as the baby has been crying and giving Esther sleepless nights. The kindly health visitor is as much concerned about Esther's own thinness and weakness. In the evening, Esther takes her daughter and one son to a youth club, which they enjoy. Later, sends the girl to borrow two slices of bread.

Saturday: *The giro comes. Immediately repays her debts.*

Esther's week, like much of her year, consists of trying to find a phone that works, collecting children, walking to numerous agencies, asking, borrowing and worrying.

Poverty of this nature leads to a continual worry over necessities. The Bradshaw and Holmes research established that the long-term poor frequently go short of clothes, footwear, food and normal participation in community activities. It means that the children often cannot afford school trips, outings to the zoo, holidays. In a nation in which some sixteen million holidays are taken abroad each year, around ten million citizens cannot afford a holiday at all.

The combined pressures of material anxieties, the feeling of exclusion, inadequate diets and sometimes damp housing can undermine health. Poor families have a much higher rate of bronchitis, pneumonia, chronic sickness and even death. In 1990, a baby from the poorest families was twice as likely to die in the first year of life as one from more affluent homes. As the government's Health Educational Council had to conclude, 'However poverty or social disadvantage is measured, the link with ill-health is clear and consistent.' In turn, ill-health becomes another drain on poor families' economic, physical and emotional resources.

Continual exposure to such poverty can undermine child-rearing methods, and it is here that a link with juvenile delinquency is found. The seminal research in this respect was carried out by Drs Harriett Wilson and Geoffrey Herbert who compared a sample of large poor families with those in better circumstances. It is research that I know well as my wife, Annette, was the research associate who interviewed all the families a number of times. As expected, the poorer families did contain far more children convicted of offences. Less expected, the parents were found to be full of care for their offspring, concerned about their progress at school, anxious that they should not get into trouble with the police. In short, the values they held were very similar to those of most other parents. So what went wrong?

It emerged that the low-income parents did tend to use child-rearing practices which were unhelpful. They were inconsistent in applying discipline, varying between repressive and permissive approaches. They participated less than most parents in the play and educational activities of their children. As the children grew older, they let them out on the streets for long hours where they were sometimes led astray by delinquent peers.

Here, then, was a research puzzle. The parents wanted the best for their children and understood that they needed consistency, encouragement and praise. Yet they were using child-rearing methods which inhibited social and educational growth, which ill-prepared the children for handling relationships at school and work, which did not teach them how to deal with authority. In short, they were laying the eggs of possible future delinquency. Why?

Wilson and Herbert explain that the parents were in such poor circumstances that they could not put their child-care wisdom into operation. In small apartments with thin walls, a premium was often placed on keeping the peace so as not to annoy neighbours. So often the parents gave in to the children's demands for sweets and crisps just for the sake of quiet. The children thus learned how to manipulate their parents. Yet at other times, the parents remained firm. Inconsistency.

In overcrowded rooms in flats which did not possess gardens, it was a relief if the children did play outside and such a release soon became a habit. Moreover, the parents could rarely afford the books and toys needed to stimulate the children nor the fares and entry fees to take them on regular family outings. And holidays were almost unknown. As the researchers put it, in somewhat academic language, 'The scarcity or total absence of toys and equipment suitable for play and the absence of privacy allowing intensive play prevent the development of creative activities, powers of concentration, manipulative skills, and the reenactment of experiences in imaginative role play.'

The children then fell behind at school and the parents, after early enthusiasm, stopped attending parents' nights where they felt inferior to others. In turn the children rejected school where they were often seen as trouble-makers. Sometimes they also got into trouble in the streets where they were picked up by the police. Parents losing control; teachers deeming the children as problems; the police frequently involved. The eggs of delinquency were hatching.

The Wilson and Herbert study has been confirmed by subsequent research. Long-term and intense social deprivations appear to push some parents into adopting child-rearing practices of which they do not approve. Yet they can see no alternative—'Oh, have the sweets then, just give me some peace,' 'Go and play outside, I'm trying to clear up.' In time these immediate responses become the built-in, usual methods of bringing up the children.

Every year I take children to holidays. One camp is in Norfolk and involves an eight-hour coach trip from Glasgow with excited nine- to fourteen-year-olds. Initially we leaders keep calm, tactfully sort out arguments, reason with the naughty ones, produce games, comics, books and crayons. As the hours go by our patience begins to wear thin. We start to shout, we no longer reason, we have no new games and books, we threaten and punish, we hand out sweets, we tell children to go to sleep so that we can have some rest. In a small space of time our initial ideas of good practice have disappeared and we have adopted short-term methods of keeping the peace. And if I had been a parent in continual poverty I would probably have done the same on a long-term basis.

Social pressures drastically affect the way parents behave, and this in turn affects the behaviour of their children. Poverty-stricken parents are in circumstances and conditions which mean that sometimes they

- ◆ cannot always express love,
- ◆ cannot constantly stimulate the social and educational growth of their children,
- ◆ cannot always provide good role models.

Further, they may then adopt practices which

- do neglect the children's material and emotional well-being,

- do entail erratic discipline,

- do lead to disruption.

In short, poverty can conceive those very child-rearing practices which make some children more vulnerable to delinquency.

Poverty does not automatically lead to delinquency. But there is a connection, and it is not surprising that those parents subject to the worst social deprivations are also at greater risk of having children who commit offences. Noticeably, lone parents are frequently poor parents, and 90 per cent of lone parents are women. Women who continue to care for their children after divorce or separation often find themselves in reduced economic circumstances. They lose their husband's salary and may have to give up work themselves. If they do continue in a job, they probably face child care costs for the minding of their children. Many such mothers, along with other single mothers, turn to Income Support— indeed 70 per cent of all lone parents are dependent on it. They fail to gain from the Child Support Act of 1991 which makes absent fathers pay maintenance for their children, for any money collected is deducted from the mother's Income Support. Poverty amongst lone mothers is extensive and in 1994 over two-thirds of their households received less than £100 a week.

To be sure, not all lone parents are in poverty—some are even millionaire princesses. And, even amongst the poor, many lone parents do bring up and adequately look after their children. Nonetheless, poverty makes parenting that much harder for single people already trying to cope without a partner. As the mother of Robert Thompson, one of the convicted boys in the James Bulger case, put it, 'They always blame the parents but it is a very difficult situation when you are getting no support and you face the world alone.' One reason why a disproportionate number of juvenile delinquents appear to come from single parent families is that a disproportionate amount of poverty is their lot. Crime does have some association with poor people but perhaps it should also be stated that, in an affluent society, it is socially criminal that so many people are condemned to poverty—and then treated as if this were a crime.

The copers

The surprising factor is not that some poor children become delinquent but rather that so many do not. For years I have run youth clubs in areas of social deprivation. As the years roll by and the hair grows grey and thin, I have seen lively twelve-year-olds grow into teenagers and then young adults. For many, their background contains many disadvantages: home in a tenement block; parents surviving on state benefits; few opportunities for travel; drugs a constant temptation; almost no prospects of a satisfying career and not much of a job of any kind. Yet the majority do not end up in prison. The same is true of poor families in general. They may be at greater risk of having delinquent children but many overcome that risk. Why?

I notice that poverty is not always a constant state, and that for some it comes and goes as parents get work, lose it, and get taken on again. In an increasingly unstable job market it is likely that this pattern will grow. However, it does mean that in the good times some families have incomes which then tide them over the bad times.

Then I've observed the importance of the wider family. Some low-income families are sheltered from the effects of poverty by aunts, uncles and grandparents who provide furniture for the home, take the kids on holiday, make loans in times of crisis. They contribute stability and so give the parents more chance of coping. By contrast, the most vulnerable are lone parents, re-housed on an estate where they know nobody and who appear to have no kin to whom they can turn in moments of despair. So differences occur within the category called 'the poor'.

These factors stem from personal observations. Three other factors, more rooted in research, also explain why some poor children do not become delinquent.

The first is very strict parenting. Wilson and Herbert followed up their research families for six years and, at the end of the period, noted that although the majority had adapted to long-term poverty by the child-rearing methods already described, a significant number responded in the opposite direction by exercising strict, almost severe, discipline and close supervision over their children. Fearful of the influence of the neighbourhood, they insisted on knowing in detail just where their children were going and with whom. They refused to let them roam unaccompanied; they set down tight rules about the times they had to be in. Some kept their children indoors nearly all the time to prevent them mixing with delinquents.

Wilson and Herbert found—and other studies in Liverpool and Glasgow confirm their findings—that these families were much less likely than others in their neighbourhood to have children who offended. Their task was a difficult one; faced with children who pleaded to go out, who felt crammed in by small rooms, who wanted to wander around like other children. This very close chaperonage could mean that the youngsters missed outside activities, lacked the enjoyment of street play, had few friends and became unpopular. The style of parenting could also be resented by the children as they grew into the teenage years. The parents were opting for a hard course, one which more affluent parents do not have to take, for they can exercise supervision with the aid of larger homes and gardens and in combination with many outside leisure activities and trips. But it seemed to work, for Wilson and Herbert recorded that mostly such parents did succeed in steering their children away from crime.

The second factor is the influence of schools. Studies of schools within the same inner-city areas have established significant differences in the number of offences by their pupils. Reviewing the studies, two leading researchers, Michael Rutter and Nicola Madge, writing in *Cycles of Deprivation*, conclude, 'The findings suggest that characteristics of a school play some part in determining how many children become delinquent.' The educational attainment of children is important, for it provides self-satisfaction and greater prospects of employment. Some teachers do possess the capacity to draw the very best out of pupils. Also it appears that the models of behaviour set by staff, responsibilities given to pupils, positive relationships with parents, all set the tone of a school which can reduce the delinquent potential of some children.

Third, the children themselves. There are children from the poorest backgrounds, whose siblings are in prison, who, against all the odds, steer clear of trouble. It is hard to explain why. An analogy with football is helpful. Football is dominated by rich clubs like Manchester United in England and Rangers in Scotland. They draw large crowds, have superb stadiums, can spend millions on new players and enjoy enormous triumphs. In the lower divisions, the poor clubs attract little support and, with everything against them, have little success. Yet sometimes they beat a top team in a cup tie. In 1994, little Raith Rovers won the Scottish league cup. Occasionally, a non-fancied team progresses through the leagues to the premier division. It is hard to explain why. Individuals play above themselves; the team clicks together as a unit; it responds to an inspirational manager. And their achievements are good for football because they demonstrate that success does not wholly depend on multi-millionaires backing already rich clubs.

It is the same in families. Life is not pre-determined, it cannot be completely explained by experts, cannot have all its outcomes predicted by theories. Individuality can overcome unpromising circumstances. Sometimes youngsters from the most difficult backgrounds do find a way out.

Some become attached to youth clubs which provide a regular and positive outlet for youngsters from crowded homes. Some obtain the sensible friendship and guidance of adults outside the immediate family—aunts, uncles, grandparents, priests, ministers. Some experience a religious conversion which has a profound effect on their attitudes and behaviour.

Some youngsters can even mix with delinquent friends yet not be drawn into delinquent behaviour. They somehow develop means of remaining popular while resisting social pressures. I've noticed that boys who are good at sport, particularly football, earn a local status which ensures their acceptance even if they will not join the gang in fighting and nicking. I see other youngsters who acquire skills of joking and humour which likewise enables them to avoid pressures to conform to delinquency, while saving them from becoming the victims of violence and bullying. Individuality can overcome.

Poverty is widespread in Britain. It can be concentrated in geographical locations which attract drug-dealers, loan sharks and other criminals. It can mean unemployment which spells a futility and despair which leads some into criminal outlets. It can create such intensive pressures that parents adapt with child-rearing methods that adversely affect their children. Poverty is thus linked with crime. But it is not an unstoppable force that inevitably drives all poor children towards crime. Many, if not most, parents manage to steer their children away from it. Youngsters themselves frequently adopt personal strategies to keep out of trouble. Poverty is a millstone which drags some—but not all—into the sea of delinquency. However, the millstone can and should be released. Society can and should combat poverty.

I made my way up the street. On the right were over-crowded, damp tenements. On the left was a flat where a teenager had been murdered in an argument over drugs. People stood queueing at the van. Most people dependent upon Income Support cannot afford cars to take them to shop at the superstores where food is cheapest. Instead they have to pay higher prices for the more limited range of goods in the vans, the mobile shops. The rain became heavier but the kids continued to play in the street. It is easy to become gloomy about the fact that these children are more vulnerable to becoming delinquent than others.

Yet I could feel hopeful on two counts. Some of the blocks were being refurbished with central heating and draught-proof windows which would reduce damp and cut heating costs. Despite its own limited budget, the local authority did want to take action. Then I walked into a room full to the brim with residents, ranging from pensioners through to teenagers. They had come to the AGM of a community group. They discussed means of providing youth and other community facilities. Many low-income people do want to uphold family life and to create strong communities. Their involvement is necessary but not sufficient. It must be backed by others outside—by citizens, by churches, by national voluntary societies, by political parties, who will determine to reduce and abolish the millstone of poverty and, in so doing, also reduce the levels of juvenile crime.

FIVE

What They Say

So far I have drawn upon research, academic observation and my own experience to outline the nature, extent and explanations of juvenile crime. But what of the views of the offenders themselves? Something can be gleaned from two sources: occasional books written by adults looking back upon their youthful behaviour; and surveys which directly question a sample of young people.

Pauline

Pauline is now an adult who has lived through poverty, the removal of her children from her care, and imprisonment. She is also a woman who, partly through the support of the organization ATD Fourth World, has found internal healing and external stability. After settling down, she was able to write about her experiences in a pamphlet called *Families of Courage*. Here are some extracts from her writings.

Before I start writing about my parents and my brothers and sisters, I want to say one thing clearly; I love my family.

I love my parents, you can't blame them for the things that happened. I think they have done their best; they wanted the best for us, like any other parents want the best for their children.

My mother, she had a rough life. Often she had to take jobs in warehouses, shops or cleaning jobs, to make ends meet at home. And at home things weren't always very easy.

Next to the jobs she had, she did the housekeeping and often went to jumble sales to get clothes for us. I used to hate it really because everybody knew that our clothes came from the jumble sale. Like coats for instance, my Mum used to make them fit me and I always took them off as soon as I was out of her sight.

There were times when I couldn't understand why my mother stayed with my Dad. She left him a few times, but she always came back and she didn't want us to say a bad word about him.

My Mum used to have a lot of trouble with me and my brother Pat and she'd have to sort things out for us. There was so much on her mind all the time. Looking back at it now, I don't understand how she managed to keep us together as a family.

My father's work was painting and decorating. He worked quite a lot but there were also times that things went wrong, when he lost his job and started drinking.

I liked my Dad in the weekdays when he was a different man, but at the weekends he was a frightening person to be with. Every weekend without fail, my Dad would come back home drunk. When we were indoors and had the wireless on, my Dad would come down from his bed and knock hell out of all of us. We used to hear him coming and we were all frightened. We often ran out of the back door before he was downstairs and tried to hide in the garden. My Mum often cried when he was like that and I used to feel sorry for her and want to protect her...

My bother Pat is one year older than me. I was really close to Pat. He was the same as me. If he didn't get attention, he would do something to attract it. He was doing mugging when he was about eleven. The first time he stole, it was from my mother because he needed money.

Once I went out with him and he mugged this lady. He took her purse and everything. I just stood there; I didn't know what to do. The lady was shouting, 'He's took my purse!' And I just stayed there next to her. It was my own brother who had done it. I didn't tell anyone. I was so ashamed of what he had done.

Pat was in a special school because he needed help. He hated the feeling that people were watching him getting into the school coach and because of that he never used to go. He turned out wayward, stealing and that. That's why he was finally taken into Care.

When Pat was taken into Care, things got worse for me, because then I had to look after my younger brothers and sisters on my own. There are three of them; Caroline, Colin and Sharon...

After that I started to play up at school. I always challenged the teachers and they used to stick me in front of the classroom where the blackboard was.

I didn't have a uniform there either and the headmaster kept threatening me with what would happen if I didn't get one soon. I always needed things for school but my mother couldn't afford it. At school they were always telling me that I had to get things and my mother kept saying to tell the teachers that she couldn't afford it. In the end I threatened my mother that I wouldn't go to school if I didn't get the things I needed.

I can remember one day at P.E. I had my period and I didn't have a P.E. kit, so I was just wearing the skirt that I wore all day long. The teacher ripped my skirt off in front of the whole class. I just got hold of her hair and swung her around in a temper. I really did lay into her. She did it in front of the whole class! That really hurt me. Another teacher had to come in to get hold of me. She wanted to take me to the headmaster, but as soon as she let go I ran out of school up to my parents.

I often got the cane. Sometimes I got it in front of all the others during Assembly. They probably wanted to give an example of what would happen if you behaved badly.

That's how it was during my schooldays and the more they punished me, the worse I got. I became more and more aggressive towards the teachers and I also started to play truant...

They put me on probation for playing truant. I didn't want to go to school any more. My parents couldn't prevent it either. I used to act as if I was leaving for school and then sneak in again through the back door and hide in a cupboard until my parents had left for work.

I had to see those probation people every two weeks. I just went to tell lies to them. They could never help me with my problems because I never told them anything. This woman used to ask me all these questions about what I had done at school and things like that. I had a social worker as well but I just wasn't interested in them. They even put me into Care for a while because nobody could do anything with me.

I never gained anything out of school. When I was at school, I used to worry about whether my Dad would be drunk again, what he would be like when I came home, or I worried that something might have happened to my Mum. There was so much on my mind all the time that I couldn't think straight anymore.

When I was fifteen, I got chucked out of school for good. They couldn't do anything with me. I was just uncontrollable.

Pauline's character and behaviour were moulded by her upbringing, by the child-rearing methods used by her parents, by the atmosphere in the home. The frequent arguments between her parents, the violence of her father, the occasional break-ups between the parents, all had profound implications for Pauline. She could never be assured of constant, reliable, unconditional love and care; she worried deeply about what was happening in the home and particularly about the safety of her mother; she lacked satisfactory examples of how to make relationships and how to deal with difficult situations. By the time she went to secondary school, Pauline was emotionally insecure and not equipped to deal with adults in authority. Her behaviour had become characterized by emotional outbursts and a tendency to seek refuge in flight.

All this occurred within a context of poverty. At school, Pauline suffered the stigma and shame of not having the dress and possessions held by most other children. Her reaction tended to be aggression and flight. She had not incorporated satisfactory ways of handling discipline, so she fought it and then truanted. But such behaviour only brought her to the attention of probation officers and social workers—she had started on what is known as a 'welfare career'. On being expelled from school, her volatile character led her into more trouble and eventually into custody. Her story is an illustration of how the combination of parental conflict and social deprivations lead to child-rearing methods which hinder rather than promote children's emotional, social, educational and moral growth.

Marian

The 1939–45 period of war, for all its horrors, is sometimes looked back upon as a golden age when the nation pulled together, people made sacrifices for each other, honesty prevailed and children behaved. Certainly, sacrifices were made but it must also be added that delinquency actually increased. A report published in 1943 by the Women's Group on Public Welfare bewailed the rising tide of juvenile crime and noted that '27.6 per cent of the persons arrested for all indictable offences were 16 years of age or less and 21 per cent were of elementary school age.' The crimes committed by juveniles were mainly simple ones against property. As a child who lived through this period, I must confess to some mini-misdemeanours myself.

Marian Hughes had a wartime childhood but did not feel she could write about it until 1994. The reason is clearly that it was also a traumatic childhood. Her father committed suicide. Her mother soon remarried but her husband was soon sent abroad with the armed forces. The mother suffered bouts of mental illness and the family lived in squalor. Marian writes of this time when she was aged eleven or twelve.

It was now evident, even to me, that there was something wrong with Mother. When she was happy the sun came out, but often she would suddenly change and the least thing made her fearfully angry. She would lie in bed for days. She couldn't be bothered to provide food but would send Dorothy out for cigarettes. Dorothy would plead not to be asked to go out.

One day, I was chasing Anthony through a vegetable market. As I ran, I grabbed at the fruit, scattering some in the process. The shouts from the stall-holders spurred me on as I raced wildly, breathlessly depositing my haul into Anthony's outstretched arms. Just two apples yet Anthony's face fell. 'That's stealing!' he cried. 'You stole them!' 'Oh Anthony! It's just fun,' I remonstrated. 'I'm hungry.' I placed my arm on his, but he shook it off. I felt a lump in my throat. 'Oh Anthony please, don't be a prig!' I cried almost bursting into tears. 'Oh come on.' He cast an anxious glance towards the market, took the apples from me and bit into the biggest one, offering me the other as we raced away from the scene.

That was the beginning.

Marian continues, a few months later:

My immediate thought was food. Cigarettes and food! For weeks now we hadn't had a proper meal and for at least two days we'd had nothing at all.

… It was now dark. The shops had closed and very few people were moving about. Feeling defeated and unable to go home without at least the cigarettes, I sat upon the steps of an elegant house with my head cradled between my arms. After a few minutes of inactivity I began to feel cold and was about to move off, when I heard someone with light steps approaching. The moon was full and bright. A little old lady drew near. As she passed, I was suddenly mesmerised by a glint of light reflected from the clasp on her handbag.

The tiny light drew my eyes as it briefly flashed through the railings, then disappeared. Swiftly rising, I silently darted after her and grabbed at her bag. Immediately she let out ear-piercing screams, one after the other. With incredible strength she clung to her bag. Then she lost her balance and I saw her face, like a little round disc of moonlight. A mask of toothless terror screaming! I let go in horror, turned and ran, the shrill cries pursuing me.

Marian was caught, taken to a police station, put into a residential institution and then sent to a foster home in Wales. After three months she ran away and, incredibly, walked back to London where she found her mother entertaining soldiers. The soldiers left; her mother retreated into bed. Marian continues.

Now and then Mummy would get up for a few days and somehow acquire some money. I made it plain that I was disinclined to steal. As the bounty left by the soldiers dissipated, we needed a minimum of food. Mummy didn't care about food and wanted to spend our very limited funds on cigarettes, which brought bitter irrational arguments between us, threatening possible violence. In the end, driven by hunger and the need to pacify Mummy's special need, I succumbed. At first I lifted just this and that, but eventually stealing once more became second nature to me and I found it easier than ever...

Twilight and a winter fog once availed me of a much-needed opportunity. In the otherwise deserted streets, I happened to spot a man by the open back doors of his van. He was peering at a piece of paper and then towards the elegant houses on the other side of the street. He marched off with a box, and I swiftly and neatly deposited many cartons of groceries into the old pram and silently disappeared into the fog. The pillage, which included cigarettes, caused Mummy to bounce out of her bed and we ate and giggled as we imagined the poor fellow in the act of discovering his loss...

Somewhere in Hammersmith, I found myself walking my [stolen] bike through a street market. A man with a colourful patter was extolling the virtue of second-hand bicycles. He eyed my rather smart racer with envy, offering thirty shillings for it. In no time, I had his money and a promise that he would buy others if my friends would wish me to act on their behalf. This became a new source of income. It was easy at the time and I gave little thought to those I robbed.

Eventually Marian was caught by the police and sent away again. Anthony too went to approved school and later to prison. The whole story is movingly told in Marian's autobiography *No Cake, No Jam: A War-time Childhood*.

Marian did know the difference between right and wrong. She read the Bible and understood the Ten Commandments. But three factors drove her to steal. One was the weakness of her mother, who either turned a blind eye to her misdeeds or else directly encouraged them. The second was her mother's lack of supervision so that Marian was allowed to roam at will. The third was the desperation arising from poverty. For all her need, her mother would not turn to the authorities for help. She feared both the stigma of the Poor Law and also the likelihood that the involvement of officials would lead to the removal of her children. Consequently she relied upon occasional gifts from men friends and what the children brought in. Marian was so hungry that she stole to eat. Hers was truly the crime that stemmed directly from poverty.

Marian's exploits occurred fifty years ago. How relevant is her experience to today? In their research, David Farrington and Donald West asked offenders why they committed their offences. Over half—50.9 per cent—frankly admitted that they stole for material gain. I too have met this response. One evening, half a dozen teenagers discussed the topic in our home and argued that, as they possessed very little, they were justified in stealing from the affluent. On another occasion, a teenager, whom I was trying to persuade to turn from delinquency, knocked on my door and asked for food. I supplied it, but to my surprise he responded in anger, 'It's alright for you. When you're hungry, you just have to go to your freezer.' He was right. I had never experienced the depths of material need sufficient to drive me to crime. The responses of these offenders confirms the analysis put forward in the last chapter. A lack of essential goods or pressure to have the same material resources as others does push some young people in the direction of crime.

Graham

Graham Gaskin's mum committed suicide when he was nine months old. He was put in the care of Liverpool City Council and thereafter his life consisted of children's homes, foster homes and periods at home with his father. He did little wrong in a legal sense until, as a fourteen-year-old, he ran away from a residential establishment and lived rough near his dad. He was known as Gazz and his old mates soon found him, as he recounts in his life story, *Gaskin*:

My best friends were Fitzie and the Dunn brothers, Stevie and Jimmy, all of whom lived in Andrew Street. Jimmy was older than Stevie by two years, but was much smaller. In fact he was tiny, but possessed of a restless, almost creative energy when it came to stealing. It was with these three that I did my first burglary, a warehouse at the back of my father's house. We threw a chunk of concrete through the window and the big shards slipped slowly to the ground, landing with a deafening crash. Scrambling in, we grabbed the first things we saw, four suitcases, and dashed out and back over the wall with them. The Dunnies' house was nearest so we took them there.

Our round of burglaries continued. One night we did the main G.P.O. building in Walton Park Road, breaking in through a side window. While Fitzie and the Dunns were looking through the parcels I went after the Registered Mail, but found it to be locked up separately in a little office. There was a basket of Recorded Delivery stuff outside so I went through that instead. The first envelope I opened contained a rentbook with £9 in it, which I hastily stuck in my pocket before the others could see. They did this, 'sticking down' as we called it, all the time when we were thieving.

'What's that, Gazzer?' Jimmy Dunn said, quick as a flash.

'Nowt, lar.' I tossed the empty book over. 'Just a bleedin' book.'

In another envelope I found a ticket for that year's Cup Final, Liverpool versus Newcastle. Later I sold it to another kid for £10 so I missed the match. Liverpool won as usual, three goals to nil.

Gazz, Graham Gaskin, was eventually arrested by the police and later served time in approved schools and prison. Many reasons account for his behaviour. He experienced disruption, deprivation and deficient parenting. But the immediate push into delinquency came from his friends, friends who knew the ropes. From his early teens, Gaskin mixed with a peer group that was highly delinquent. It was a company that gave him acceptance, a sense of belonging, status. But the price of entry was to adopt their values and criminal behaviour.

The influence of peers is powerful. Recently I drove some parents to collect their sons from the police station after they had been caught shoplifting. One boy, who had no previous record, clearly felt that that he had had to act the same as his mates in order to retain their approval and to avoid being rejected as a wimp. This boy and Gaskin are both examples of the influence which peers can wield. They are not isolated examples.

West and Farrington's survey, recorded in *The Delinquent Way of Life,* revealed a small but significant number of respondents who said that they were drawn into delinquency by the pressure of the company they kept. They did not want to be different. Two Home Office researchers, David Riley and Margaret Shaw, interviewed 750 teenagers and found that boys who reported having friends who committed offences were over seven times more likely to be delinquent themselves. It should be added that the company which youngsters keep cannot be completely isolated from the influence of their family. Parents play some part in guiding their offspring concerning choice of friends. But, as the youngsters get older, the power of their peer groups gets stronger.

Vic

Vic Jackopson was one year old when his father died and his mother deserted him. He then went through a childhood of children's homes until he was fostered with a couple with whom he felt very happy. Yet soon he was stealing from them. He recounts the story, taken from his autobiography, *From Prison to Pulpit*.

What made me start stealing from the home of the two people I loved I will leave for the psychologists to debate. I remember well the first of many occasions. Mum Smeeth kept her well-worn handbag in the bottom of the kitchen cabinet. I waited until I could hear her cough from the bedroom above. Down into the bag I delved pocketing some of her Craven A cigarettes and a half crown from her purse. The old man who had come to live at the Smeeths was the first to suspect my light-fingered habits... [He] exposed my misdemeanours... and insisted that it was a matter for the police to deal with so I was taken round the corner to receive a severe warning from the Station Sergeant who was an old friend of Pops.

Then Vic turned to house breaking, and developed the ability to write authentic-looking letters to play truant from school.

It was ironically the Smeeths who uncovered my daytime activities. I had been to the scouts that evening following a successful afternoon of housebreaking. As I sat on the kitchen table listening to the radio Mum Smeeth playfully snatched at a comb which was protruding from my pocket. As she pulled it out along with it came a bundle of notes.

'What's this?' she cried, startled at such a huge sum of money.

'Oh, I was minding that for Mr Tear the scoutmaster,' I answered, hoping that that my quick-witted reply would satisfy her now obvious suspicion.

'Get into the car dear,' said Pop as he clasped the money. 'We must take this back at once.'

As I heard the car pull away from the house I realised I had been caught red-handed. They would get to Thornhill and within ten to fifteen minutes would be back with Mr Tear and probably the police too.

Children in public care can have positive experiences. But the disruption to their lives can bring questions, doubts and experiences unknown to most children. They question why their own parents do not look after them, may even blame themselves for a death of a parent or a break-up of a marriage, may wonder whether they are unlovable. In Vic's case, the disruption led to experiences which damaged the way he reacted and behaved. Moved from place to place, he never gained a sense of security. He lacked the feeling of being loved for himself. He was never given explanations of why he was in public care. He never experienced a close relationship with adults who concentrated just on him. Consequently, by the time he did move to a foster home he could not handle relationships with loving adults. He felt so unlovable that he seemed to seek rejection and punishment. He thus acquired ways of behaving which eventually led him to a prison cell. It took a conversion to Christianity, dramatically told in *From Prison to Pulpit*, to change his attitudes and behaviour.

Boredom

The accounts by Pauline, Marian, Graham and Vic may not be typical. They are by youngsters who spent long periods away from their parents and who as adults developed the skill of writing. Yet their stories do serve to demonstrate the effects on children of experiencing various combinations of parents who cannot cope, absent parents, intense poverty, unhelpful peer pressures and disruptions. One other factor, perhaps not so powerful as these, but still an inducement to crime, needs to be mentioned—boredom.

I recall a youngster saying to me, 'I was with some friends, we were bored, there were some stones and some windows in an empty house, so we broke them; all this happened because we had nothing to do.' The offence was minor but the boys were prosecuted and obtained a criminal record. More seriously, some of the youngsters involved in disturbances on council estates in 1993 and 1994 attributed their participation to the boredom and monotony of their lives. In the survey published by Farrington and West in 1977 some 19.2 per cent of offenders pinpointed boredom as a reason for their delinquency. That by Kate Painter in 1994 reported 79 per cent putting forward this explanation. Perhaps the increase is connected with the sharp rise in youth unemployment in these years.

The main factors

The explanations arising from the autobiographical accounts and from the questions put to youngsters in surveys confirm those of the research studies discussed in previous chapters. The main factors pertaining to juvenile crime can now be grouped under the following four headings.

The family

Certain aspects of family experiences, or lack of it, can steer some children towards delinquency. They are

♦ **DEFICIENT CHILD-REARING METHODS**
Parents who are unable to provide their children with constant affection, stimulation, consistent and fair discipline, and good models of behaviour, are not equipping them with the capacities to relate with others, to develop their educational and social skills, to cope with authority, and to form the kinds of values which tend to hold them back from illegal behaviour.

♦ **CONFLICT**
Frequent arguments between parents and between parents and children appear to provoke distress and unhappiness which, in turn, adversely affect

the children's behaviour. Simultaneously, the children may adopt aggression and fierce argument as their means of meeting needs and wants.

♦ **DISRUPTION**

Children whose lives are disrupted by separation from one or both parents, by frequent moves between different carers, by removal into public care, do not necessarily become delinquent. But they are at greater risk than children whose lives are marked by stability. It appears that traumatic and frequent changes can be interpreted by children as a rejection of themselves. Such inward damage can reinforce the negative effects of any deficient child-rearing experiences.

Poverty

Clearly, poverty is not *the* cause of crime, for many poor children do not become criminal. But social deprivations can make the victims more vulnerable to delinquency in the following ways:

♦ by leading to a desperation which drives some to steal or use other illegal means to obtain basic resources;

♦ by creating a boredom and sense of futility which finds outlets in unacceptable and damaging behaviour;

♦ by making adequate child care more difficult for parents.

Social environment

Children whose backgrounds dispose them towards delinquency may be precipitated into it by features of their immediate social environment, that is, by the people with whom they mix and by the institutions which they attend in their everyday lives. In particular, they may be drawn into crime by their peer group, by the example and pressure of friends who encourage them to steal, shoplift, housebreak, fight, and so on.. Or they may attend schools which are not effective bulwarks against juvenile crime.

Public values

Crime does not occur in a vacuum. It can be sanctioned by prevailing values or by public models of behaviour. Some sections of the media do exalt violence and certain sexual crimes. Some public figures, particularly those in politics, may display a greed and corruption which other citizens then emulate.

The above four factors do not operate as separate entities. A poverty-stricken family whose child-rearing practices are undermined by their social deprivations may also find themselves living in a neighbourhood where a gang of delinquents adversely affect their children. A child whose parents are always in conflict may also take refuge in video programmes which stress violence and cruelty. A teenager, bored by unemployment, may reason that if certain public figures break the law to get money, then so may he. There is no single explanation of delinquency and hence there can be no single solution.

PART TWO

ACTION

CHAPTER
S I X

Prevention Before Punishment

Juvenile crime is harmful to its victims, its perpetrators and to society. What can be done about it?

In the wake of some horrific crimes, the early 1990s saw calls for more punitive measures. *The Daily Mail* in a 1994 editorial headed 'Time to get tough with young thugs' advocated greater use of custody for persistent offenders. The editorial followed policy moves by the Government. In 1993 the then Home Secretary, Kenneth Clark, proposed privately-run secure units and a new secure training order for young criminals. The case for greater use of, and harsher types of custody was continued by his successor, Michael Howard, whose praise for a 'get tough' approach won him much applause at the Conservative Party's annual conference. Ultimately, although faced with much parliamentary opposition, he succeeded in passing legislation in the Criminal Justice and Public Order Act 1994 for five secure training units, each taking forty youngsters in the twelve to fourteen age-range.

The move to lock up more young people reflected a trend amongst adult offenders. Between December 1992 and December 1993, the proportion of offenders jailed by the Crown Courts rose from 40 per cent to 52 per cent, with the prison population reaching a record high of nearly 50,000.

The role of custody

Custody must have a place in any justice system. Some people are so violent, so criminal, that their liberty must be removed in order to protect other citizens. Imprisonment has to exist as the punishment for those for whom all other measures have failed. But the basic debate concerns how quickly, at what age, and for what crimes, offenders should be put behind locked doors.

Imprisonment may protect potential victims and punish the wrong-doers. But does it, as successive Home Secretaries claim, actually help the inmates by providing them with training which positively improves their characters and behaviour? The evidence for the success of any kind of institutional care suggests not. Even taking children into public care, which is not usually a criminal procedure and is done for the best of reasons, can have unforeseen and unfortunate results. Children in care tend to underachieve at school and have a higher chance of unemployment than others. They are eleven times more likely to be charged with an offence than children who are not in care. Moreover, a national prison survey conducted in 1991 found that 38 per cent of prisoners had spent part of their childhood in public care.

Public care often involves removing children from their families but is not the same as being in custody. What is the effect of containing youngsters in custodial institutions? In terms of outcomes once they are discharged, the results are not promising. Cairine Petrie's follow-up of boys who had been in a Scottish List D (approved) school and in a high security unit revealed that two-thirds re-offended within a short time of being released, and most of those ended up back in custody. The most recent Home Office figures reveal that 85 per cent of young men and 49 per cent of young women aged fifteen to sixteen who had been in youth custody establishments were re-convicted within two years. For males aged seventeen to twenty-one, the re-conviction rate was 82 per cent within four years. The

names given to institutions change with the years—
approved schools, community homes, detention centres,
training centres, borstals—but the results in terms of re-
offending are always the same. The reasons are not
difficult to understand: once inside the offenders mix
with other criminals and so learn more about criminality;
they are cut off from their own families and communities
and so, on release, find it difficult to settle down. The
experience is well illustrated by the words of a youngster
describing his experience in an approved school, taken
from David Rose's 'The messy truth about Britain's violent youth' in *The Observer*, 28 February 1993:

*I was in shock most of the time. I was stuck in a place where all
the kids were as f—ed up as I was, and these staff had to control
us. Yes, we had our activities, our games, our visits to the
swimming baths. They gave us merit badges when we were good.
But there was no love there, no emotional growth. It was an
institution, my first prison... I learnt everything about crime
there. I did my first burglary one night when I ran away. I learnt
how to drive, how to steal a car: how to fight and how to lie and
get away with it. It made me what I am, it was where the criminal
subculture started. We got together there and formed relationships
because we had nothing else.*

Soon after his release from approved school, he was back
inside at the age of fifteen in a detention centre. He
continues,

*They turned us into little tough guys. There was circuit training
every day, and a lot of physical abuse from the staff. And again you
met all the lads who'd been to approved school, through the courts
system, who were already dreaming of a career in the big time.*

*And the more they tell you you're bad, you're a criminal, the
more you accept it and get on with it. At DC, kids were already
seeing themselves as gangsters. That's where you made your
connections, and found out what families from what areas are
into what type of crime, and how to sell your goods.*

Later he went to borstal and then prison.

Qualifications must be made to these dismal findings. Take public care. I started my social work career as a child care officer and know that some children have to be removed from abusing parents or parents who cannot cope. Once in care, they may be looked after by skilled and dedicated staff or foster parents. But overall, the results are not promising. Children may even suffer abuse while in public care, as recent scandals have shown, though these are exceptions. Much more likely is that the children will suffer a number of moves, in addition to facing the difficulty of understanding why their own parents could not look after them. It is not surprising if their educational potential is not reached and if they do badly on the job market. It is not surprising if numbers do become offenders. How much better if their removal from their families and their subsequent experiences had been avoided by preventative practices, thus enabling their parents to cope in a satisfactory manner.

It is a similar story with those youngsters who have been in custodial care. The system does contain many staff who have the interests of children at heart but their devotion can come too late. The task in residential establishments has become ever more daunting. Staff are trying to meet the needs and demands of youngsters whose lives are already severely damaged, who may be herded together with other offenders in isolation from the rest of society, to which they return with the label of criminal stuck upon them and with all the odds stacked against them on the employment market. How much better if their childhood experiences had been such as to prevent them developing into youngsters who later had to be sent away. And today, surely, it would be more sensible to spend the estimated £100 million needed to establish five secure training centres on measures to remove the need for such centres instead.

The demand for locking up young offenders is a powerful one. But there is a danger that the calls for harsh punishment spring from anger not tempered by reason. The MP David Evans claims that, 'Society is breaking down on the streets' and asserts that the solution is more custody with 'a rigorous deterrent regime, corporal punishment in schools, hanging for murder and the return of national service'. It is easy to dismiss him as a man whose excessive income from his business interests and his MP's salary detaches him from life at the hard end. Yet I too can react with anger.

A boy in our district was recently made fatherless when his dad, a train driver, was killed in an accident caused by vandals. When we heard the news, my wife and I both raged with the hope that the youngsters responsible would be put away for a long time. In fact, we did not know if it had been youngsters who had placed concrete on the railway line: and, if it was, we did not consider whether they were unemployed young people embittered with their lot in society and whose misdeeds might have been prevented by policies which created employment.

Anger is understandable and sometimes justified. But it cannot be the sole basis for social policy. The response to someone like David Evans is to agree that action is necessary but to argue that custody is rarely effective in changing behaviour. It might also be added that corporal punishment had little beneficial effect on the likes of Pauline and Graham Gaskin, whose exploits were described in the previous chapter; that hanging is not a deterrent; and that there was no connection between national service and the reduction of crime. Policy must be based on an analysis of what works in combination with a desire to uphold justice in society as a whole.

The argument here is not that delinquents should not be punished. Rather it is that policy should concentrate resources less on locking-up regimes, which are known to be counter-productive, and more on measures which prevent children reaching the point where locking up is considered necessary.

Prevention

In a previous book, *Putting Families First*, I discerned two sides to the preventative coin. There is reactive prevention, in which action is taken once a crisis occurs. And then there is positive prevention, which ensures that crises do not arise. For instance, a youth worker perceives that trouble is brewing on the estate where he works and that a gang of teenagers is plotting a violent raid on a youth club in a neighbouring territory. Just before the appointed time, he persuades the youngsters to accompany him to a pop concert: the trouble is avoided— reactive prevention. The same youth worker has helped establish a parents' group where members are taking an Open University course on parenthood while their small children benefit from nursery care: the hope of the youth worker is that these children will develop in such a way as not to need violence and crime as an outlet—positive prevention.

Can delinquency be prevented? It will never be abolished but the explanations put forward in previous chapters suggest that much could be avoided. Much delinquency has its roots in unsatisfactory family experiences. It follows that if parents are helped with their child-rearing practices, that if families are enabled to reduce conflict and disruptions, then more children will grow up with the means to cope satisfactorily with life. Other delinquency is associated with factors outside the home which are likewise able to be changed—by providing opportunities to divert young people away from trouble. And parents and youngsters would be helped by a reduction in poverty, by an increase in employment, and by public values which uphold family life and honesty. Prevention, both reactive and positive, is possible.

The main responsibility for prevention rests with local authorities. The Children and Young Persons Act of 1963 placed on them a duty to prevent children having to enter public care and to diminish the need to bring children before a juvenile court. These responsibilities have been confirmed and extended by subsequent legislation, particularly the Children Act of 1989 which states in Part 3, section 17,

It shall be the general duty of every local authority...
(a) to safeguard and promote the welfare of children within their area who are in need; and
(b) so far as is consistent with that duty, to promote the upbringing of such children by their families, by providing a range and level of services appropriate to those children's needs.

Later, in the same act (Schedule 2, section 7), it is made clear that local authorities have a duty to 'encourage children within their area not to commit criminal offences'. It should be noted that much of this Act does not apply to Scotland which is awaiting its own child care legislation.

Local authorities, particularly through their Social Services Departments (SSDs) and Social Work Departments (SWDs) in Scotland have adopted some preventative strategies using personnel such as social workers, family aides, welfare assistants and intermediate treatment officers, and agencies such as day nurseries and juvenile justice bureaux. Particularly worthy of mention are family centres, which expanded during the 1980s. Family centres are community-based agencies which offer services such as day care, parents' groups, counselling, and welfare rights advice to families.

Other local authority departments also play a part in prevention. Local authority youth services may make direct provision of youth facilities and give grants to voluntary bodies to do so. Education Departments, as mentioned, can make a crucial impact on delinquency by the quality of their schools at nursery, junior and secondary levels. Reference should also be made to the Probation Service which, via the courts, supervises some young offenders within the community. Along with SSDs, the Probation Service has also organized Intermediate Treatment schemes which provides constructive outlets for groups of young people who are, or who are in danger of becoming, delinquent. In England and Wales, the departments work closely with the youth courts and in Scotland with the Children's Hearings system.

Obviously, statutory bodies are the lead agencies in preventative work. But their efforts are nowhere near sufficient, for the following reasons.

Insufficient resources

Since 1979, government policy has been to restrain public expenditure. One means to this end has been to limit the scope of local government. Consequently, numbers of local authorities, faced with rate capping if they exceed expenditure limits set by government, have had to make cuts. In particular, services for the under-fives and youth activities have suffered. In addition, there is concern that changes brought about by the Education Reform Act of 1988, whatever its other benefits, will reduce the attention that teachers have previously given to combating delinquency. Thus the introduction of the National Curriculum and the devolved management of schools, along with the opting-out of some schools, has put pressure on schools to demonstrate academic success and to do well in league tables in order to attract the most able pupils and to win extra grants.

The fear is that schools now have less time and fewer resources for the less able pupils—those who are most likely to turn to delinquency. David Utting, in the Family Policy Studies Centre's report, *Crime and the Family*, reports that there is 'a serious rise in the number of young people who are being excluded from schools.' If given less attention, such children may turn to disruptive behaviour and, if excluded, may be left to their own devices for long periods in which they seek excitement by offending.

The growth of demand

In the last decade, poverty and unemployment has risen sharply. Local authorities have thus found themselves under increasing pressure from poor citizens who need their services. Social deprivations can also stimulate more crime, and its perpetrators and victims are also likely to turn to the local authorities. Thus at the very time when local authority expenditure is being restricted, the demands on its services have escalated. The result is that services have not been sufficient.

Changed priorities

SSDs and SWDs, faced with financial problems, have had to prioritize their work in ways which do not favour positive prevention. Media attention on child abuse, often linked with criticisms of social workers, has led many departments to shift the bulk of their child care resources towards the small but very important number of children who are believed to be in immediate danger of abuse and neglect.

The outcome has been less emphasis on long-term supportive services to families whose problems are not yet so dramatic. Thus Gibbons and her colleagues in their study *Family Support and Prevention*, found social workers in 'a retreat from their earlier commitment to prevention'. A survey by the National Council of Voluntary Child Care Organisations reported that SSDs were not carrying out their obligations under the Children Act towards children 'in need'. Their failure was not due to a lack of intent but, as the Association of Directors of Social Services pointed out, arose from a shortfall of between £100 and £150 million for such children.

Family centres show what is happening. They were established mainly as neighbourhood services which attracted a wide range of parents who could be given support and advice at an early stage in a non-threatening atmosphere. The pressure of child abuse combined with insufficient resources has meant a shift towards family centres which cater just for those families with immediate child abuse difficulties.

As well as local authorities, the national voluntary societies, especially the child care ones such as Barnardo's, NCH Action for Children and the Children's Society have played a distinguished role in developing preventative services. Yet they too are experiencing financial strain and, in order to win contracts from local authorities, may have to tune their services more in accord with the theme of child abuse as favoured by the statutory bodies.

No one doubts that the lead in prevention will continue to stay with statutory bodies and the huge national voluntary societies. But their limitations, shortages and priorities now leave gaps which may have to be filled by smaller, more local organizations.

This book is not aimed primarily at professional welfare staff, academics and experts. Its intention is twofold: to stimulate discussion of the reasons for juvenile crime; and to suggest means by which local organizations—churches, community groups, neighbourhood associations—may devise and offer preventative services. Their small size and lack of statutory clout may seem obvious disadvantages. Yet they may have a credit side. Local residents are the ones who can best perceive the needs of their area, can spot the lack of appropriate services and can identify local resources and strengths which can be utilized. Further, being ordinary, low-key and voluntary can mean that they do not convey stigma.

Stigma means a sense of social disgrace. The Poor Law deliberately stigmatized its recipients by restricting their liberties, making them do degrading work and marking them out as social failures. Far from being helped, those stigmatized usually responded with a withdrawal or an aggression which only reinforced their plight. Such stigmatizing does not occur today but clients of the statutory social services can still feel they are marked out as criminals, delinquents, child abusers. Their resultant sense of inferiority can make them reluctant to receive help or, curiously, can sometimes goad them into the very behaviour which puts them beyond help. Local projects which carry no legal powers, which cannot remove children or liberties, may be well placed to operate without conveying any such negative connotations.

Prevention and prediction

Given that resources are limited, on whom should prevention be targeted? In recent years, some academics have developed the skill of predicting which children will become delinquents. Already previous chapters have shown that certain children are more likely to commit offences later in life. The study of children in the north-east found that 70 per cent of children assessed before the age of five as being both economically deprived and receiving poor domestic care were eventually convicted of a criminal offence. Other research claims that teachers in junior schools can spot future offenders by their aggression and disruptive behaviour. Accordingly, John Patten, when Home Office minister of state, urged teachers and welfare workers to pick out the future criminals, saying: 'We want to identify these youngsters... before they reach the stage where they will face punishment.'

Is the best approach, then, to single out the predicted delinquents and then to focus resources on them in order to prevent their march into criminality? Attractive as this method seems, the answer must be 'no'. Predictive techniques can be very unreliable. In the sample used by Donald West and David Farrington, 71 per cent of boys who came from low-income homes, whose parents had poor parenting skills and who were criminal themselves, did eventually become delinquents. But, obviously, 29 per cent did not. Further, far more boys in this sample who did later commit offences were not identified. Allocating resources on the basis of prediction would mean that some children would be treated as potential offenders although they were not in fact at risk, while a large number of future offenders would be missed out.

The method also contains a danger. If children are predicted as delinquent, if they are treated as such, if teachers and social workers expect them to cause trouble, if they interpret all their behaviour as a confirmation of their predictions, then it might well be that delinquency is unnecessarily thrust upon them. Certainly, they will carry the stigma of delinquency. It follows that the distribution of resources on this basis of identifying delinquents might actually reinforce the problem.

A better approach is to offer services to neighbourhoods where delinquency rates are high. However, the target should not be delinquency as such. Instead, the aim should be to provide resources which strengthen the communities and families as a whole but which in so doing also help to undermine the development of delinquency.

For example, comprehensive youth provision in an inner-city area will be to the benefit of a cross-section of youngsters. Within that number will be some potential and actual offenders who can gain help without being publicly marked out as the predicted ones who are seen as criminal and dangerous. Clearly this method entails expenditure on young people who are not at risk of future trouble. However, the justification is that they too should be able to enjoy good youth services.

In Part 1, it was argued that delinquency often has its roots in family malfunctioning, often in association with poverty and conditions of social deprivation. It follows that preventative programmes which carry no stigma could concentrate on these key growth stages:

The young years

Parents are under most stress when their children are young. Children's characters, personalities and behaviour patterns are most significantly shaped during their early years, particularly the years nought to five. It makes sense therefore to target some resources on young , low-income parents with young children.

The environment years

Once they start school, children become much more influenced by outside forces, by their social environment. In the early school years, school and home are the powerful influences. As they grow still older, they spend more non-school hours outside the home, playing with friends, mixing in the streets. Peer groups become increasingly important and it is during these years that some children will have their first brushes with the law. Notably, the largest proportion of children in public care are in the age-range ten to fifteen years old. It follows that preventative efforts could make some impact by offering programmes and activities for youngsters in this age group.

The delinquent years

The teens are the peak period for criminal activity. But even once some teenagers have committed offences, it is still possible to take measures to attempt to change their behaviour—reactive prevention. Diverting delinquents within a context of wider youth work is another, albeit challenging, form of intervention.

Such programmes and projects aimed at families and young people are necessary but they cannot operate in a vacuum. Parents, children and youngsters also require strong communities which support, not handicap, home life; they need to be free from poverty, in a society which puts a premium on honesty, fairness and integrity. It is not claimed that voluntary groups, clubs, churches, community groups and neighbourhood associations can transform communities, can abolish poverty, can change public morality. But they can make a contribution, as the last chapter in this book will suggest. The plan for the remainder of this book is therefore to give examples and to make suggestions for activities which can help the following:

- ◆ pre-school children and their parents (Chapter 7);

- ◆ vulnerable parents (Chapter 8);

- ◆ school-aged children (Chapter 9);

- ◆ teenagers: most of whom will be located within low-income neighbourhoods (Chapter 10).

Then attention will be directed at national issues. It must be stressed again that this book is not about statutory social workers, probation officers, police persons and prison staff who tend to tackle crime after it occurs. It is rather about how non-statutory bodies and concerned citizens can stimulate facilities and conditions which help to avoid delinquency taking root. The aim of the projects and programmes which will be described in the following chapters, therefore, is not limited to preventing delinquency but will also include ways

- ◆ to stimulate the social, educational and emotional growth of young children;

- ◆ to encourage parents, particularly low-income parents, to develop positive child-rearing methods;

- ◆ to provide facilities for school-aged children which are an attractive alternative to anti-social behaviour;

- ◆ to divert away from delinquency those teenagers who have taken initial steps along its path.

All these ends are worthy in themselves. Their attainment will also simultaneously help to reduce juvenile crime.

SEVEN

Laying the Foundations—the Early Years

The early years of children's lives are crucial to the formation of their personalities. Their capacity to make satisfying relationships, their performance at school, their career prospects, even the odds on them becoming delinquent all have at least some roots in their pre-school years. Of course, parents are the most important figures in the upbringing of children but, especially after the age of about two, experiences outside the home become increasingly significant. Consequently, the contribution of organized care at this stage—often called day care—has been recognized as one of the foundations of child development.

In Britain, there are various types of day care. Not counting childminders or supervision by relatives, the main kinds of pre-school provision are as follows.

Local authority day nurseries.

Run mainly by Social Services Departments, day nurseries provide full or part-time care for children aged between one-and-a-half and four. Often the children are referred by social workers or health visitors while the parents pay a fee after being means-tested. The staff are trained nursery nurses. Since the last war, the total of day nurseries has declined markedly and they now account for less than 1 per cent of under-fives.

Private nurseries

Private and voluntary nurseries, day care centres and work crèches have expanded of late and take about 2.5 per cent of young children. Their growth owes much to the demands of working parents who may pay between £45 and £150 a week. Similarly, private nursery schools also charge fairly high fees to provide an educational emphasis and cater for around 3.5 per cent of under-fives.

Playgroups

In recent decades, playgroups have multiplied and now contain places for about half of all three- to four-year-olds. Staff are mostly trained by the Pre-School Playgroups Association. The children attend for two to three sessions a week with fees at about £1.70 for a session of perhaps two or three hours.

Nursery education.

Local authority education departments organize nursery education either within separate nursery schools or within nursery classes attached to junior or primary schools. The education, by trained nursery teachers or nursery nurses, is mainly part-time, is free, and serves about 25 per cent of all three- to four-year-olds. In addition, some schools have special reception classes for the 'rising-fives'.

Voluntary care schemes

Despite this variety of provision, day care places are in short supply. Surveys reveal that numbers of mothers have difficulties in finding the kind of provision which suits their pockets and their children's needs and which is within convenient travelling distance from their home. Consequently there are opportunities for voluntary bodies to offer under-fives care which can be of value to young families. Many churches and other associations maintain, or allow their premises to be used by, play-groups.

Examples of pre-school provision

A small number of voluntary organizations offer more extensive care, of which two examples are given here.

The Tot-Spot Crèche

St George's and St Peter's Church of Scotland Church is located in the midst of the vast council estate of Easterhouse in Glasgow. In the late 1980s, its minister, the Rev. Malcolm Cuthbertson, called together a meeting of church members and other local residents to discuss how the church property could be of more use to the community. The outcome was the formation of the St George's and St Peter's Community Association which soon established a number of activities open to the neighbourhood. One of them was a crèche for young children in one room in the church hall. The demand for day care was so strong that it expanded and is now run by qualified staff in a spacious nearby building.

The atmosphere in Tot-Spot is that of relaxed order. The children have the use of two, large, brightly-coloured rooms and enjoy activities planned and organized by its two qualified workers, the leader, Kim Watson, and Helen Morris. Each weekday, forty children, aged between one and five years, attend either for the morning or the afternoon session. Kim and Helen are assisted by Employment Trainees who receive training in child care and a small wage. When I visited, ten trainees, male and female, were playing with and teaching the children. Tot-Spot is about to take over a third room which will be converted into a well-equipped kitchen, making it possible to provide lunches so that some children can then stay all day.

The children's parents identify strongly with the crèche and have their own Parents' Room. They meet socially here and can also attend courses aimed specifically at women, such as self-defence and assertiveness training. A few are enabled to work part-time, although jobs are scarce in the area. In the summer, parents and children enjoy outings to the zoo and parks while a holiday takes place at the holiday centre which is run by the Community Association at the seaside.

Most of the money for Tot-Spot comes from an Urban Aid grant from central and local government. This is topped up by fund-raising in which the Parents' Committee plays a strong part with dances, welly boot contests and raffles featuring regularly. Parents also make a donation of £1.50 a week for their children. Recently, Tot-Spot has been awarded a grant from Children in Need to turn the land outside into a playground.

Tot-Spot is inspected and approved by the Education Department and its reputation is such that it receives many requests to take students for placements. Yet it remains a local project, run by staff who reside in the area, and serving the needs of the neighbourhood.

The Handsworth Day Care Centre

During the 1960s, the inner-city area of Handsworth in Birmingham became noted as a location of both social deprivation and ethnic unrest. A third of its households had no indoor toilet, a third no bath; and over 12 per cent were large households with six or more members. A committee of the local adventure playground observed that many parents could not find suitable day care for their small children. Eventually, after a public meeting, a committee was formed to promote the Handsworth Day Care Centre which started in a large house rented from the local authority. Over a quarter of a century later, the centre still exists and has expanded into two houses, one for children aged two to five and another for those aged five to eight. The rooms are brightly coloured and are divided into different sections with paintings depicting their particular functions—art room, reading space, dressing-up section and so on. The nature of the work is revealed in the following interview with Fiona Dodd, its deputy director.

We have twenty-four children aged two to five, all Afro-Caribbean. We open in the day care side at 7.30 a.m. and go on until 5.45 p.m. There is a long waiting list. People hear about us from health visitors or social workers or by word of mouth. Some have had a previous child here and put down the name of the next one as soon as she or he is born. We give some priority to those referred by social workers or health visitors for a special reason, like the child's behavioural or speech problems or if the parents are finding it difficult to cope.

Everybody pays. There are nineteen assisted places which means that the social services pays although the parents still pay £10. Others pay £50 for the week.

The staff consists of a director, deputy director and nursery nurse who all have the NNEB [Nursery Nurse] qualification, one who is studying for her nursery nurse qualification, and an unqualified but experienced worker. These are for the younger children. For the older children there are three play-leaders, all of whom have done the play-leaders course. In addition, there are three auxiliary staff as cooks and cleaners.

On the two- to five-year side a typical day is like this. When the children come in we have table top activities with constructive and imaginative toys or jigsaws or colouring. At 9.30 a.m., by which time all the children are here, we have breakfast. At 10 a.m. we have general activities which we all plan in advance as a team: some will be doing water play, others painting, music, dough play etc. At 11.15 a.m. we play outside. Then the children divide into two groups and have stories and singing time. Next it is dinner until 1 p.m., followed by the mat session in which some children sleep or do quiet activities. At 1.45 p.m. we have milk time, then outside for half an hour in the garden. We come back inside for table-top activities, followed by another story-time then tea-time. From then on it is free play as the children gradually are picked up to go home.

I think the children benefit much from coming here. They mix with other children and with adults outside the family. They really get ready for school, for we have a high educational content and give them pre-school work. Also they learn what is socially acceptable and not acceptable, that is, they learn the kind of behaviour which adults—and other children—will not tolerate. We get a lot of good reports from the schools who say that children who have been here do much better at school than those who have not. It is a head-start. I think too we prevent abuse, for there are no children on the abuse register.

In the other house, we have the out-of-school scheme for five- to eight-year-olds. They arrive before school, from 7 a.m., and we take them to school, pick them up again and keep them here until 6 p.m. Then the same children can come here in the school holidays. The service is open to anyone in the community and costs £20 a week in term-time and £38 a week in holidays. Obviously, it is mainly used by parents who are at work.

The centre is run by a committee which is elected annually. All the parents can vote, as can other supporters. Two places on the committee are set aside for parent reps selected just by the parents (one from the two to five side, one from the five to eight side). All the committee members live in the area and include some former parents. One house is rented from the council and the other from a housing association. We get two grants from the SSD, one for the day care, one for the out-of-school project. But we have to fund-raise as well.

We are a community-based project with staff, children, parents and committee being rooted here. We get all our supplies locally and shop-keepers deliver it and involve themselves in the centre. They bring presents for the children. The community policeman comes in. They all join in at Christmas and come to watch our children do the nativity play.

The value of day care

Many non-statutory bodies do, or would like to, offer some pre-school provision to their neighbourhood. Just how important is it?

Day care with unmotivated staff, too few staff, poor supervision and inadequate equipment will have little positive effect. In 1994, an investigative television programme revealed unsatisfactory practices in some private nurseries with children in unstimulating conditions and staff who sometimes gave them little attention. On the other hand, there is little doubt that varying kinds of day care are of benefit, provided that they are well run, comply with local regulations and are in accordance with the Children Act 1989. They will be of value for these reasons:

Play

Good day care provides children with the opportunities, materials, company and stimulation for play. And play is an essential part of child growth. In 1994 a report was published, chaired by Sir Christopher Ball, called *Start Right. The Importance of Early Learning*. It stated,

Play is a primary vehicle for learning. Through their play children develop intellectually and also physically, emotionally and socially. Play gives children a sense of control in which they can consolidate their learning and try out developing skills and understanding.

Progress

Day care is often associated with children making educational progress once they start school. However, the evidence also suggests that these early gains may tail off as they get older unless reinforced by continuing and stimulating educational input.

A model for parents

It is not just the children who benefit. Sometimes day care provides a much needed respite for parents, particularly lone parents, who are under stress. Moreover, as Utting and his colleagues make clear in their study, *Crime and the family: Improving child-rearing and preventing delinquency*, day care staff may also constitute good models of child-rearing who, for instance, handle children in consistent, non-aggressive ways and who demonstrate the value of play. He adds that their influence can be particularly important when they draw fathers into playing a fuller part in the care and upbringing of small children.

A way out of poverty.

Not least, accessible and moderately priced day care can be economically beneficial to some parents. Utting again points to government research in Australia and Sweden which establishes that state-subsidised day care not only reduces national income differentials by allowing poorer people to take employment but is also a means of reducing state expenditure as they give up welfare benefits. In Britain, some 1.25 million children could be taken out of poverty if their mothers could find the day care to allow them to work.

So various kinds of day care have various benefits to the advantage of children and parents. Probably, in some cases, they promote in the small children the values, skills and behaviour which will later act as a counter to delinquency.

However, there is one kind of day care in which high-quality research has demonstrated beyond questionits effectiveness in preventing juvenile crime—High/Scope.

High/Scope

The Perry Pre-School Project in the USA, which became known as High/Scope, is probably the best known and certainly the best researched project on nursery education. It involved 123 children drawn from poverty-stricken African/American families who received a pre-school programme and who were compared with a control group who did not. Unusually, the study followed them until they were twenty-seven years old. The programme, applied to three- and four-year-olds, involved daily two-and-a-half hour sessions for five days a week. It was characterized by being applied by trained teachers, with a ratio of at least one teacher to ten children, who put an emphasis on allowing the children to choose their own educational activities within a structured learning programme.

The school programme was supplemented by weekly visits of one-and-a-half hours to the parents in order to ensure their participation in the children's education. By the age of twenty-seven the results were striking. Those who had received the pre-school programme had performed better throughout their school careers, earned more at work, were more likely to own their own house, were less likely to have contact with the social services and—crucially as far as this book is concerned—were far less likely to have committed crimes. In all, only 7 per cent of the study group had been arrested for five or more crimes, as against 35 per cent of the control group. The outcomes are clearly seen in the following table (source: Schweinhart, L.J, & Weikart, D.P. (1993), as reproduced in Utting et al (1993), *Crime and the Family: Improving child-rearing and preventing delinquency*, Family Policy Studies Centre, London).

Table 2 Comparison between pre-school group at age 27

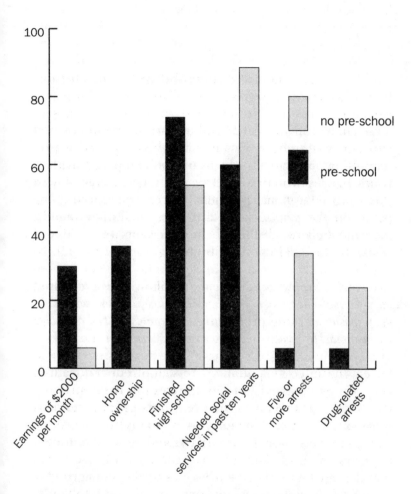

What was it about this pre-school programme that proved so crucial? The experts agree that it instilled motivation, social skills and confidence. The children chose and planned their own education and play and were enabled to carry through their intentions. It gave them mastery over what they chose to do. As they grew older, they continued to respond to challenges and difficulties with confidence rather than with apathy and defeatism. As the Ball Report so aptly puts it,

The second great commandment teaches us to love our neighbours as ourselves; more concisely and memorably than modern jargon can, these words identify the fundamental importance of self-esteem and social cohesion for the well-lived life. They are also essential for successful learning.

The High/Scope research is confirmed by studies and experience elsewhere. Quality pre-school education gives many—certainly not all—children a confidence and mastery which enables them to co-operate with others and to achieve their own educational potential. In consequence, they do better on the job market. Relationship skills, educational attainments, jobs, all these help youngsters keep clear of crime. As the Ball Report sums up,

Good early learning socialises young people; it reduces the risk of later juvenile delinquency... Together with parental education, the provision of good early learning is arguably the best available means to tackle crime. Prevention works better than cure.

Given the effects of quality pre-school education, it is surprising that provision is not greater in Britain. Fewer than half of three- to five-year-olds attend nursery schools or classes, whereas in many of Britain's European neighbours it is well over 90 per cent. Indeed, as nursery education is a permissive and not a mandatory duty of local authorities, there are signs that current financial restrictions are forcing some to cut it. Of course, education for the under-fives which provides the kind of programme just outlined, using trained staff and a good staff/child ratio, is expensive. Yet the High/Scope research also showed that for every $1 spent, another $7 was later saved in reduced spending on special education and crime.

Pre-school activities of various kinds are likely to be

beneficial, and it is not surprising if hard-pressed voluntary groups have given most attention to play-groups and mother and toddler groups which are both useful and cheap. Yet the pay-offs from nursery schools and day care centres—in allowing parents to work and reducing delinquency—are so great that it is hoped that churches and voluntary bodies in deprived areas will promote them more actively. A few settlements (local voluntary establishments which originated from middle-class people settling in deprived areas) and community centres have maintained nursery schools. The examples of St George's and St Peter's Community Association and the Handsworth Day Care Association show that local groups can run good quality day care with trained staff. Moreover, there are charitable trusts which have a special interest in nursery education.

Family centres

Day care provision concentrates on providing healthy foundations for small children with some involvement from their parents. Family centres—of the kind developed by voluntary bodies to serve neighbourhoods—are more focussed on the parents, usually mothers, as well as providing services for children, in order to strengthen family life. Family centres are hard to define but their aims, methods and coverage will become more clear as two are described. In the first example, I use the words of the participants themselves; in the second, I describe a family centre which I visited.

The Walcot Centre

The Children's Society, formerly the Church of England Children's Society, is a national charity which, in the 1980s, pioneered family centres in areas of high social deprivation. For eleven years I worked for one of the centres and also had opportunities to visit others. One which I admired was the Walcot Centre, housed in a pre-fab building on an estate in Swindon. Its objective was defined as 'to involve local people in projects which are designed to improve the life chances of children from the area in which we work'. The centre's staff consisted of a project leader, an under-fives worker, two neighbourhood workers (one part-time), a welfare rights worker (part-time), an administrator (part-time) and three nursery nurses (part-time). The following accounts, researched for an earlier book of mine, *Putting Families First*, tell how the workers, a user, and an outside professional who knew the project, described it.

Project Leader*: My work as project leader is mainly concerned with administration and groups. The groups range from the staff team, the training groups of volunteers, to a new group we are starting for claimants. Occasionally, when someone else is not available on a particular crisis, I will see local residents directly, but generally I work through staff and volunteers... Sometimes the volunteers have faced severe problems themselves, like a woman who lost a baby through a cot death and was helped by being in touch with a group. But there are a diversity of volunteers and that has the advantage of a diversity of approaches.*

The project has been based on AIR, Accessible, Informal and Reciprocal. Accessible does not mean that the centre is open five days a week. It means that someone is available. There are now networks of informed individuals who through training or commitment have knowledge of community and social services and who are identifiable within their own streets. Informal means that we respond without an appointment—no need to fix a time in coming here. Reciprocal implies that people can give something back. If you visit the centre, it is hard to know who are the staff, the volunteers and the users, because everyone is mixed in together.

There is something about being local and accessible which means that we may be more likely to deal with crisis situations than a local authority SSD in the centre of town. Often the centre staff are the first port of call. This means we can be preventative in terms of keeping children out of care. But we do more, in terms of empowering local residents, increasing self-confidence and self-esteem, and increasing the involvement of local people in identifying their own needs.

Under-Fives and Families Worker: *My main responsibility is the Acorn Project in which I lead a team of four. In the beginning I worked closely with the health department in the baby clinic and set up a group called Clinic Link, which helped isolated parents with young children to make friendships. During one of these sessions the health visitor expressed her concern that many families did not attend the clinic. Our ideal became a special playgroup with high health input where parents could share in the play and growth. The Children's Society and the health department agreed to a two-year pilot scheme. Acorn was born...*

Acorn is for children twenty months to three years old and the group opens two days a week. We start with free-play sessions and parents work alongside staff, helping their children by naming objects in a book, fitting shapes in a puzzle, or helping to build a child's confidence in climbing and balancing skills. The parents have a rota where they help the cook prepare the midday meal and learn about cooking and the nutritional value of the food children eat. The parents take coffee breaks together; this enables them to build friendships in the group. If parents have problems, are feeling low or upset, the family worker is available to talk things through.

We have formal teaching for the parents in the sense of discussing films on child development and behaviour. The doctor and health visitor are available to talk to parents individually about children's health problems, contraception, breast feeding or parents' health. We have fun things too like parents having their hair done or beauty treatment at the local college or going to the local ice-skating rink.

We are preventing children coming into care, preventing abuse, preventing them falling further behind in development. One parent here was sent by the social services as a last chance before they took her children away. She left the children alone for hours on end, shut in their rooms, with no stimulation, no warmth, clothes not changed, poorly fed, their bottoms all raw. I thought she was going to be so hard. But she's lovely, she really likes coming. We cannot force mums to come but we have only ever had one who dropped out. Mums come to support each other. One mother was in and out of psychiatric hospital and the other mums were really supportive; they looked after her children so the husband could visit her. Mums who left a year ago still meet together on their own, go to their children's parties and so on. In the summer we hold play schemes and the old mums come back. The fact that the mums come from the same neighbourhood means that they keep on seeing each other and they go on to the same playgroups and school together.

Neighbourhood Worker: *Married at sixteen, divorced and remarried, I've spent years staying at home looking after my children. Taking my younger girl to school, I saw the Walcot Centre and went to keep fit. From the outside it looked like some old hut but it was amazing inside because it was so friendly. I met a lady here and we became good friends and we went to J. (former leader) and expressed our concern about isolated mums in Walcot. We thought she would do something but she said, 'What are you going to do?' We called it Neighbourhood Care Volunteers (later changed to Family Link). Eight of us decided we wanted some training first. We got so much from the training— self-awareness and listening skills. We then contacted outside agencies for referrals to visit. Some of the referrals were devastating to us. I had a mum in a top flat threatening to throw her baby out of the window. I went with her to the housing department. Me! I had only ever been to pay the rent before. Well, when this man knew I was from the Walcot Centre he shook my hand and asked if I wanted tea. His whole approach was different from what I was used to. And it was successful. At the end of the day she had her house.*

Eventually I became a full-time worker. What Family Link can provide is one of the most important things in preventive work, that is time. It could be in the evenings, at weekends, sometimes I spend near enough the whole day with a one-parent mum who's bruised her children. Social workers are restricted in the time they can give. This mum had lost confidence, there was no bedding, just a mattress which a kid had wee'd on night after night. The mum was so depressed, I had to spend time with her and we became good friends. Gradually the little boy went to school with underpants on. Before she hadn't got up to dress him. I used to go there in the mornings to give her a knock. This is preventive work. I want to do something before the child gets battered.

I am now doing a CSS (Certificate in Social Services) course. It is a chance in a million for a mum on Walcot but I must not forget my own experiences.

Neighbourhood worker (part-time): *A number of things have helped me. One is living on the estate. When I go out on my bike, it is a matter of 'hello, hello, hello'. Another is that I know what it's like for my husband to be unemployed. Sometimes you see women outside the school all tense because their husband has been laid off and you can say, 'There is someone in the Walcot Centre that deals with welfare rights, come and see them.' Some people just cannot cope with money, with children, with life in general. Like me, they are not very good at making the housekeeping money last from Friday to Friday. You learn it is all right to have to go to jumble sales for your clothes. Also now we pass clothes around. It is sharing clothes and it is sharing a problem. I see mums standing at the school gates, their faces full of problems, and I can see me standing there six years ago. That's how I was, so I can offer them the hand of friendship.*

User: *My child wasn't thriving so the health visitor suggested I came to Acorn with her. I didn't think it would help but it has. She is pottying herself now but foodwise she is still not right.*

Last night about 11 we put a fan on to heat her room—we can't afford heat all the time—and took her up with a bottle. She began screaming. I was tired, I could really have hurt her but something in me said 'No.' I can understand how some parents do it. When I woke up this morning, I didn't want to come to Acorn. I was fed up and tired. I rang S. and she said, 'Oh, come in.' So I did and now I feel better when I talk about it instead of bottling it up. I wouldn't want my child to go into care. If the centre shut down, there would be a lot of bad things happening to the kids.

Social worker (from SSD): *It is important that the centre is not part of a statutory body. We've got statutory responsibilities and the families see us as... 'You are going to do what I want.' And that is reality. Families at risk need the kind of support that is non-threatening and agencies that can spend time with them. That is what the Walcot Centre does. It can really raise people's sense of worth. It does so by encouraging families to take on responsibilities for particular tasks. Originally they share with the families in their difficulties but gradually they withdraw. Our caseload and referrals to our department have diminished as a result of the Walcot Centre being there.*

The St Gabriel's Family Centre

St Gabriel's Anglican church is located in a working-class part of Walthamstow in East London. In response to the Church of England report, *Faith in the City*, the local vicar, John Gutteridge, and members of the church began planning for a family centre. The Diocese of Chelmsford made a grant to employ a neighbourhood worker, Caroline Gleaves, to help make the plan a reality. Much fund-raising, particularly from charitable trusts, led to an extension being added to the church by October 1992 and this became the family centre.

The aims of St Gabriel's family centre are stated as follows,

We aim to improve life for local children by recognising the role of parents. We thus provide a range of activities which include groups for children, groups for parents, and groups that the whole family can attend together.

We aim to find ways to relieve pressure on family relationships often caused by housing, low income and ill health. This may involve helping people to negotiate with statutory agencies, enabling them to take a break, providing information or encouraging the development of new skills.

Under the management of the Parochial Church Council, along with a support group for Caroline Gleaves, the centre has furthered these aims in three directions. First, there are groups directly run by the family centre itself. These groups cater for many different needs.

The Buggy Brigade is for children under five and the people who look after them in the day time. It has a planned pattern of stories, music and play both inside and outdoors. Toddle-In is less structured and involves parents and young children meeting together. There is also a café which is open every weekday both for participants in the groups and for those who just drop in. An aerobics class with a qualified leader has been a popular draw. Youth clubs are held one evening a week, having sections for three- to nine-year-olds, ten- to thirteen-year-olds, and fourteen and over. In addition there is the Girls Friendly Society for girls aged six upwards. These clubs—like the weekly worship service and women's meeting—have a definite Christian emphasis, for the committee feels a responsibility to witness to the Christian faith while also opening the doors of the family centre to residents of other faiths or no faith at all. Finally, the elderly are not forgotten—there is the Good Companions Over 60s Club and Friday Fellowship dinners for those who usually eat alone.

Second, there are groups run by outside agencies. Circle Bereavement uses a small room for counselling purposes. A local special school brings in its pupils once a week to enjoy the excellent play equipment. Training for childminders, along with a crèche for their children, is also a regular feature. Parent Link is another voluntary body which helps some needy parents develop their child-rearing skills. Interestingly, mothers who have completed its course now meet together in their own Parent Support Group. Neighbourhood Crèche is another gathering of twenty local parents who organize themselves to come together with their children once a week. The bright, airy, rooms in the family centre are also hired more occasionally by an Alzheimers' Disease Support Group, the Tenants' Association and a Money Advice Service. They are also used for birthday and other celebrations.

Third, individual work. Caroline has got to know many residents in the area and sometimes helps them negotiate with statutory bodies, such as the housing department, gives advice on welfare rights matters, and accompanies them to court or tribunals. In addition, the SSDs, the housing department and the police sometimes refer needy people to her so that she can give practical advice on family and child care matters. In particular, she has become a link with newcomers re-housed in the vicinity from hostels.

For the future, the members of the family centre wish to extend its outside play area and also provide a sandpit and tricycles so that more local children, many of whom live in tower blocks, can have use of safe and stimulating play facilities. They also plan to install ramps in order to improve the access for children (and adults) with disabilities.

St Gabriel's Family Centre receives no statutory funding. The centre has been built and a neighbourhood worker employed by money raised from the church, from trusts and from local people. It makes much use of volunteers to run popular services for many families while its premises also provide much needed facilities which are used by other agencies.

The value of family centres

The two family centres described above are typical of others run by voluntary bodies. They have attracted a great deal of interest and some study. The Children Act (1989) specifies them as agencies which can give support to families. The research conducted to date is not as rigorous or long-term as that applied to High/Scope but the studies are increasing in number and their findings have a general agreement. They reveal that family centres have a four-fold value:

First, they succeed in attracting disadvantaged families yet without conveying any sense of stigma. Some family centres will not accept referrals from statutory services for fear that users may be put off. Instead they are just open to anyone in their neighbourhood. Users mainly went to the centres because they were near to their homes, because friends introduced them, because the services they provided seemed relevant to their needs, because they walked in and received a friendly welcome. Even at the Walcot Centre, where some users were referred by official services, there was no pressure on them to attend and they mixed freely with other users who had not been asked to go there. The centres thus draw in needy people who tend to come in a receptive frame of mind.

Second, the programmes, the activities, the groups which parents attend do appear to improve what the researchers call 'child management skills'. The parents, mostly mothers, learnt from the staff, from volunteers and from each other. They did so by:

♦ observing the behaviour of others—for instance, how others stimulated children's play;

♦ asking advice from individuals—for instance, about how to deal with bedwetting or temper tantrums;

♦ joining in courses—for example, an Open University course geared towards getting parents to encourage their children in their education. Nearly all the studies mention that users tend to grow in self-esteem and here a link can be made with High/Scope, for just as children need the confidence to meet challenges and master their environments, so do parents.

Third, the parents are strengthened by their engagement with each other. Isolated parents, especially lone parents without the support of relatives or friends, can be at their wits' end. The groups they attend at the family centres, the friendships they make there, tend to counter their loneliness. No doubt the children also gain from their involvement in activities, but the distinctive point about neighbourhood family centres is that they are as much geared towards parents. As the Ball Report says,

It is difficult to exaggerate the value of committed parents and good parenting skills. They are even more important to a child's lifelong welfare than good nursery and primary education. Parents need support and education of two kinds: in understanding the long-term and serious demands of the role, and in acquisition of the relevant skills.

Family centres appear to help parents, mainly low-income parents, in both these directions. Yet without contradicting these points, it is also true to say that some women mention that what they like about family centres is that they are not seen just as mothers. The centres give them opportunities to develop other aspects of their lives in leisure, education and training. And probably this broadening of their interests also helps them to cope as parents.

Fourth, and arising out of the above three points, family centres have a preventative impact. Crescy Cannan in her study of family centres, *Changing Families. Changing Welfare*, explains that it is 'largely current stresses in families which may tip the balance between coping and not coping' and adds that often family centres are a means of alleviating these stresses. The welfare rights advice which is available at most centres can make a difference to the income which some families receive. The availability, friendship and encouragement of staff and other participants may see some through a crisis. Their better handling of the children can ensure a happier home life. All these facets may well promote a better quality of life and, in so doing, prevent the break-up of families and the emergence of delinquent tendencies in children.

Family centres with their staff and buildings do not come cheap. None the less, voluntary agencies have maintained successful centres with the minimum of full-time staff and the maximum of volunteer involvement. Local community bodies have run family centres in partnership with local authorities and national charities. Some churches do so in co-operation with the Shaftesbury Society.

Building the foundations

Pre-school provision and family centres can lay the foundations of positive family life by supporting both children and parents. Hopefully more will be started. Yet these services will not come about just as a result of a committee decision that they are a good idea. They will require much planning and fund-raising. In addition, the social concrete in the early foundations must be of the right mix if the projects are to be successful. Three ingredients are essential right at the start:

- ◆ The new agencies must comply with national and local guidelines and regulations in regard both to what constitutes good practice and also to the more mundane but vital matters of registration, space requirements, planning permission, health and safety and fire regulations, insurance and staff ratios.

- ◆ The new projects must be sensitive to the needs and norms of the immediate community and particularly take into account the views of ethnic groupings who may wish to use pre-school or family centre facilities.

- ◆ Local participation in the initiation, establishment and maintenance of new projects must be maximized. Paternalistic or authoritarian agencies are unlikely to succeed. They must be a part of, and belong to, local people.

EIGHT

Alongside the Vulnerable—Help for Parents

Day care and family centres tend to serve a cross-section of families often drawn from low-income parents with young children. The hope is that any difficulties can be countered at an early stage.

But sometimes something more is required. It may be that the parents have been under stress for so long that their responses and energies are almost defeated. It may be that unhelpful child-rearing practices have gone on for too long a period. It may be that as the children get older they seem less susceptible to change. Perhaps the parents require more intensive, more individual help than is usually possible in a nursery group or family centre and yet are unwilling to seek official intervention for fear—not always justified—that officials will act to remove their children.

Learning to be parents

In Chapter 2, it was explained that children's difficulties in making relationships, anti-social behaviour, delinquency and so on may stem from their parents' difficulties in conveying constant love, consistent discipline, frequent stimulation and adequate role examples. Could these parents have altered their practices? Can good parenting be taught, even to those in difficult circumstances?

In 1994, an important seminar was organized in London by the Family Studies Policy Centre. Based on the work of Gerald Patterson and his colleagues from the Oregon Social Learning Centre in the USA, it set out to demonstrate how parents could learn more positive ways of dealing with children even though they were some years into the spiral of family conflicts and over-stressed relationships that can end in parents giving up and youngsters turning to crime.

The seminar explained that when approached by parents, staff at the Oregon Centre initially spend some time with them in their home in order to identify the children's demanding behaviour, such as whining, arguing and disobedience, and the parents' reactions, such as verbal or physical abuse, shouting, inconsistent methods and over-reactions, which make matters worse. The staff then draw up a chart which gives points for good behaviour, such as getting up on time or setting the table, and deducts them for misbehaviour. On reaching a certain score, the children are rewarded with treats which vary from extra time watching TV to extra pocket money. The parents are committed to spending more time with the children, being more con-sistent, less dictatorial, and so on. They also learn moderate responses such as sending children to their rooms to cool down instead of hitting them. In short, the parents take on positive discipline which comes across to the children as fair and caring.

It sounds simple but the parents are grasping something profound, namely that they had lost control and that the children's responses were making it increasingly worse for all. The new approach reverses the trend.

With twenty-five years of applying the method to families with aggressive, disobedient and delinquent children, Patterson and his team claim it is effective with 75 per cent of children aged under nine but with only 25 per cent of adolescents. They explain that the latter have accumulated secondary problems such as academic failure and membership of deviant peer groups. None the less, if the families come early enough, the team argues that their relationships and behaviour patterns can be changed to the benefit of the children's development.

It may be countered that the Oregon team consists of psychologists and therapists who are hardly likely to be in the reach of small agencies which want to set up means of help in those locations where parents are most under pressure and where children are most likely to be delinquent. But the point here is not that local associations can or should set up prestigious clinics with a staff of numerous professionals. It is rather the deduction that parents can be helped, even within those families who seem to be far down the track which ends with their children displaying severe behavioural problems. The question then becomes, are there other approaches which can both help such families and are also within the reach of the modest resources of local organizations? Two examples can be given.

Newpin

Newpin (New Parent—Infant Network) is a voluntary body which started in a small way in 1981 and now has a number of centres. It has some similarities with family centres but it tends to draw families in from a wider area and to concentrate all resources on them, whereas neighbourhood family centres serve a small geographical community while providing a variety of services. The origins, methods and scope of Newpin are well described in two articles which appeared in the national press in 1987 and 1991. The first is by Ann Shearer.

When Jackie first came to Newpin, she says, she couldn't say anything to anyone; she was scared to go out on her own. Now, her son in nursery school, she's at college. She has learned to face her fears, to negotiate, as she says, rather than simply exploding when things get hard. She plans to become a social worker, to give something back. 'I had one when I was a child. I was a date in her appointment book, that's all. I think I can do better than that.'

Newpin stands for New Parent—Infant Network, and the 450 or so mothers who have become a part of it over the past six years will understand what Jackie means. Their lives are the sort from which the statistics of heartbreak are drawn, the sort that yield the finding that up to 40 per cent of young mothers are isolated and depressed, that their children suffer disturbances in behaviour and learning. Many of these women grew up with family disruption and insecurity, and most now try to build families of their own in face of constant battles with the housing and social security—and very often without a partner to share the responsibility. They are the people of whom professional social workers say that their problems are so multiple and diffuse that it's hard to know where to start—even if they had the resources and time, which they don't.

By 1982, workers in the then Guy's [Hospital] health district in South London knew that they simply weren't able to offer the intensity of support that many local mothers needed. Take-up of antenatal care was low. Anne Jenkins, herself then a health visitor with a local general practice, knew what it was to have to leave despair untended as she grappled with that huge caseload of 300 families or more. Local child abuse statistics were alarmingly high. So Newpin was conceived, with Anne Jenkins as its coordinator, to offer a place where young mothers could drop in, with a crèche and facilities for laundry and cooking, and a base for one to one befriending of new mothers by 'experienced' ones as well.

The idea seems obvious enough. But what makes Newpin different from other schemes of its kind is its refusal to divide women into 'helpers' and 'helped', its belief in the talents of each and every individual who comes its way, and its commitment to helping them discover these through intensive group and sometimes individual explorings of past hurts and present strengths. Between the twenty-five or so families currently on its books—mostly referred by health visitors—and the roughly same number of 'volunteers' there is no firm divide. This woman may not be able to cope with a one-to-one relationship; she's encouraged to drop in and gradually find her place. That one may benefit from the twenty-two-week training programme which offers a therapeutic group on one half-day a week and on another, discussion around such potentially painful themes as giving birth alone, post-natal depression, racialism and child abuse as well as education in child development. 'Volunteers' continue to attend a weekly group for as long as they are at Newpin. Even lines between staff and the rest are blurred. As Anne Jenkins says: 'We all have a common bond. We've all been born and grow up and use our defences—whether of class, education or colour—to hide a lot of pain.'

She knows, too, herself the mother of four, that all of us live in a society that makes life harder with its constant, insidious urgings that we shouldn't trust anyone at all. 'The only person you really behave well to is the person you know—you're suspicious of everyone else, and that erodes the fabric of society. People form tighter and tighter groups—and yet they become more and more isolated.' What Newpin is about, finally, is rebuilding networks of trust, not just between individuals who may have known little enough of it, but across a community itself.

The ethos warms the crowded, battered comfort of Newpin's rooms, perched on the first floor of a defunct child welfare clinic with views across to those bleak estates. It's a second family for them here, the women often say; for some, it's the first. 'Everyone mucks in to help each other,' says Sheila, who comes each day with her small son, back with her now after the long months of her breakdown. 'The girls know when you're feeling down. They keep on at you—What's the matter?—and in the end you tell them. And Brian loves it.' Another young mother, who found herself completely alone in London after escaping from a horrifying marriage, does not know what she'd have done without Newpin. She does know how much better her boy is since they've been coming here, how much better she understands him. She's found an education, too, in the group meetings. 'It helps you grow really. It makes you aware of so many things. It helps you make up your own mind.'

People who have been around Newpin from the start say you can begin to see the change in its mothers extraordinarily quickly. There's a new confidence, an attention to dress, a way of walking.

Some early research on the project (more is being completed by the DHSS) bears them out: a remarkably high percentage of Newpin mothers, many of whom had their first child young and saw little point in schooling, go on to further education and full-time employment. Margaret Lynch, community paediatrician at Guy's and one of the scheme's originators, knows that when mothers who belong to it consult her they are far more articulate than others about what they want, far better able to manage the professionals. The confidence ripples. The children show far fewer disturbances of behaviour. Margaret Lynch cannot remember a single case where, once a mother has joined Newpin, there has been serious concern about child abuse. Anne Jenkins knows how often crises are averted by the alerting of that network of support that stretches from Newpin into the estates.

For some of the most vulnerable and isolated young families, of course, it could generate a lot more besides. As one of the mothers once said: 'I would like to pack Newpin in a suitcase and take it around to everyone and say, Have a slice of that, it will do you good.'

Four years later, Angela Phillips also wrote about Newpin as follows:

Children, whatever the ads tell us, are not angels. They are bundles of ego and energy, concerned with getting what they want out of life. Some learn to do it with charm, others by confrontation; many learn the hard way that they cannot have what they want. A few die on the way. They are the Jasmine Beckfords, Tyra Henrys and Doreen Masons, born to parents without the resilience to cope with such demands and with no understanding of why they should.

Parental abuse or neglect contributes to the deaths of around 160 children every year. Sometimes such abuse is deliberate; more often it is simply a spill-over of a life in which love, tolerance and understanding have never had much space.

When a child is hurt, society looks for someone to blame. More often than not it finds another victim, an abused child grown up to be an abuser; for mothering skills are not innate, they are learned. Doreen Mason's mother was said to have been sexually abused by her father and was in care by the age of eight. With no memories of being handled lovingly, it was hard for her to know how to deal with any of her feelings, negative or positive, for her own child. All society could offer was a social policeman knocking on the door to see if she was carrying out capably a job for which she was entirely unequipped.

Sharon McCauly (not her real name) could so easily have become another Christine Mason. 'My mother spent most of the time at bingo while my father went to the pub. Me and my sister used to play on the streets.' By the age of eight she was at boarding school. She had asked to be allowed to leave home to escape sexual abuse from her older brother. Her sister came, too, to escape the same fate from their father.

Now her sister's four children are likely to be taken away because, says McCauly, 'She hits them like I hit mine.' Her own three boys are all under six and have been on the at risk register for two years. Says McCauly, 'Jason kept getting up in the early hours, getting food out of the fridge and trying to feed the baby. I smacked him so hard I bruised him. The middle one I nearly strangled. He was swearing, kicking and biting the baby. Mum said, "Your kids are going to be taken away," and the next day the police came.'...

For over-stretched social services, the only option usually available in such a situation is to take the children away. But what Sharon McCauly needed was someone to reach through the layers of neglect and rejection that had cut her off from both professional help and friendship. Fortunately, she happens to live near one of London's five branches of Newpin. McCauly herself believes she would have lost her children permanently by now if she hadn't been referred to an organization that believes in teaching mothering skills.

At Newpin—a charity partially assisted by the Department of Health—the philosophy is that every mother can learn to value herself and her children. Director Anne Jenkins believes that had

Christine Mason been referred to the Newpin in her area, her daughter would have been alive today. At Newpin every mother has the opportunity to unburden herself, to speak out about the bad things she has done and to fan the flame, however small, of good feeling she has for herself and her children.

In the six months since her referral, the most visible change is that you can actually see Sharon McCauly's face. When she first arrived she used her dark curly hair as a screen to hide from the world; today she looks you in the eye. As she talks about her children, she no longer dwells only on how bad they are. She says she loves them and for the first time has allowed herself to consider a future that could be positive.

Another mother summarised what it is that makes Newpin different: 'When you go to other drop-ins, everyone just talks to or about the baby. Here people talk to me.'...

On the surface it is much like any other mother and toddler group but no one coming here for the first time will find herself on the outside of a clique, because all the regular supporters are trained to be sensitive to the needs of vulnerable women. In time, each of these new women is offered the opportunity of a weekly session of group psychotherapy, plus sessions in child care and lifeskills. The training is not a treatment but has an end in view. Once a woman feels strong enough, she will become a supporter herself.

Sharon McCauly's supporter, Kay, is herself a mother of four who initially joined Newpin because she was depressed and unable to cope. According to McCauly, 'Social workers are nosy. They come and look in your fridge to see if you have enough food for the children. The health visitor used to tell me to bath the kids but I couldn't be bothered. Kay is different. She helps me, she doesn't tell me what I'm doing wrong. I don't really know anything about kids or housework. Kay came round and showed me what to do. She told me that if I bathed the kids, they would sleep better and I've found they like it and they feel better too.'

Already her life has changed. ' I never used to go out. I wanted to but I had nowhere to go. Now I can come here and I've met other people. Shelley and me go to the park together. She told me she reads to her kids and Kay is teaching me to read and write better, so I can read to mine. I've found I'm cleverer than I thought.'

It isn't all easy. McCauly admits she still has trouble with her middle son who is unruly and inclined to bite, but now at least she can talk to someone who won't threaten to take her child away. In the ten years in which Newpin has been operating, not a single woman referred to them has had a child taken into care. That is the bottom line.

Newpin is successful with parents who are at the hard end, those who are frequently living in poverty. They are often lone parents who are not only poor but have also endured years of isolation and stress. In short, they possess many of the social disadvantages which can provoke the spiral of pressure which can push even loving parents into the unhelpful child care practices which, in turn, lead to child behaviour which concerns the authorities. Newpin's success is that it enables parents to adopt child care practices which help, not hinder, their children's development.

Newpin offers its users four essential factors. First, acceptance. Whoever they are, whatever they have done, the staff and supporters accept newcomers. Second, group support. Individuals comment that when they are low they can walk into Newpin and receive a warmth from people who have become their friends. They know they are not alone as persons and they are not alone in their problems. Third, training. Newpin makes no secret of the fact that its policy is to teach people to be better parents. This may occur within group sessions led by professionals or by the words of the supporters. Fourth, the acceptance, the support and the training instil confidence and self-esteem.

The High/Scope project was designed to give children mastery over the challenges they met. The Oregon approach emphasized that parents had to be in control of what they were doing. The lesson keeps coming through. Parents need confidence to achieve the practices which they know make up good child care. Yet that confidence depends on having certain social, emotional and educational skills. It is these skills that Newpin can identify and teach.

Could Newpin be repeated elsewhere? Could it be run by groups of residents in the inner cities and sprawling estates where so often other Jackies and Sharons are living and where the future of their children seems so bleak? Why not? For, unlike the Oregon Programme, Newpin does not depend upon a large team of highly-qualified professionals. It was initially inspired by a former health visitor but the essence of its being is that its support, friendships, programmes and training depend largely on two sources drawn from non-professionals: local volunteers and the mothers themselves. It is not denied that the contribution of trained workers may be crucial in the early years. But Newpin demonstrates that professional staffing can be minimized while that of volunteers and parents can be maximized. It follows that costs can be kept down so that a well-run project which successfully helps parents can be achieved within a modest budget.

Home-Start

The other example, Home-Start, like Newpin, rests on the premise that volunteers, who have parental experiences themselves, are well placed to support other parents going through periods of stress. However, Home-Start is different in that the volunteers concentrate on going to the homes of the families. Started in 1973 in Leicester by Margaret Harrison, there are now 133 Home-Start schemes in Britain. Each one is independent with its own local committee and usually a paid organizer. They all share the same constitution and contribute to the parent organization, Home-Start UK. Altogether, the schemes involve some 4,000 volunteers visiting over 8,000 families with 21,000 children. The volunteers receive some initial training and then visit, once or twice a week, families who have referred themselves or who are introduced by social workers or health visitors.

To mark the International Year of the Family in 1994, Home-Start UK published *Family Album* by Sheila Shinman (with Sue Pope and Sue Everitt) which graphically describes the work of the schemes by looking at 500 families who were seen by volunteers in the first three months of 1993. Of these, the majority were two-parent families, with 27 per cent being lone parents. Many suffered conditions of social deprivation, with 60 per cent being dependent upon Income Support and 43 per cent living in inadequate accommodation, damp, cramped and without play space. Their lives were indeed troubled ones: the children often showed behavioural problems and the parents lacked the skills or resources to cope. Two other factors contributed to the family problems: 82 per cent of the parents had experienced troubled childhoods themselves, while 31 per cent were going through current marital difficulties.

In the face of these daunting problems, what did the volunteers do? In the first few weeks, they established rapport with the parents (usually the mothers) and the children, provided transport, played with the children, helped the mothers with a specific task, such as speech therapy with a child. Within a month or so, sufficient trust was usually established for the volunteers to take the children out and so give the parents a break. By the third month, the volunteers often brought in toys and read to the children, so showing how play could be a positive, helpful and planned activity for all. After four to five months, the mothers often confided deep anxieties such as their own childhood traumas and their present relationship difficulties with their partners and children. The volunteers listened, advised, encouraged.

Often, during these months, the volunteers were also trying to break the mothers' sense of isolation. The isolation sometimes sprang from being newly housed in a tower block or, by contrast, in a distant rural area. Or it sprang from lacking relatives and friends, or from being a lone parent hemmed in by several children. Sometimes it sprang from depression, from emotional withdrawal following the break-up of a relationship, from a sense of rejection and failure. The more the mothers stayed in, the worse the problem became, with a high number finding their children put on the local authorities' Child Protection Registers.

The volunteers sometimes found that just by babysitting they gave the mothers the opportunity to go out. More often, they initially had to accompany them to the welfare clinic, the doctor, the park, a mothers' group, the cinema. In time some mothers were enabled to go on a holiday, start a training course, obtain a part-time job. To make this progress which broke their isolation, they had needed the encouragement of volunteers.

In recent years, Home-Start has attempted to give special attention to parents from ethnic minorities, to those whose children have special needs, and to very young mothers. Home-Start is determined that its practices should not deny access to families whose cultures and backgrounds are different from the mainstream. The first step was to recruit volunteers from minority groups. In regard to some Turkish, Kurdish and Asian families, the volunteers advised that meeting together at the agency's premises was more acceptable than receiving a visitor. In other instances, a visitor was welcome, as shown in the following example from *Family Album*, published by Home-Start.

A Sikh family recently moved into the area to a seventh floor in a high-rise flat. They have no car. One of the two under-fives has severe eczema and both lack stimulating play. Mother is pregnant and feels unwell most of the time. She has no clothes washing or drying facilities. She feels lonely and unsupported.

January. *The volunteer makes ten visits. From the time spent travelling, she obviously lives fairly close by. Each visit lasts about one hour. She takes the mother (and the children) to a hospital and to see her GP. She listens and reads to the children.*

She helps with housework and in building up a routine. She gives information, translates letters and helps with documents and form filling. On each occasion she offers emotional support.

February. *There are only four visits this month. They are shorter and are regular each week. The volunteer takes the mother to her hospital appointment; she helps cook and wash up. On every visit she hugs the children and takes in a new toy and activity for them. The mother's sickness has diminished and she is feeling better able to cope.*

March. *Again four visits, but they are longer—up to one hour because there has been a setback. The mother is very upset because of a racist attack and much of the time is spent hearing what happened and discussing what to do. The volunteer hugs and plays with the children on each visit and continues to introduce new activities. She also rings the mother between visits to offer telephone support.*

Home-Start members are aware of the special needs of children (and parents) with physical and mental disabilities which lead to extra financial, emotional and physical demands. Interestingly, such families may be materially better off than most who come to Home-Start's attention but they are still in need of the friendship of volunteers as this example, also taken from *Family Album*, demonstrates:

Mother is disabled (MS) and father works full time. They have two children, one with Downs Syndrome. The family live in a comfortable but rather isolated house in the country. Mother needs help to choose appropriate play activities for the children and to develop housekeeping skills.

January. *The volunteer makes one visit of two hours, equalled by her travelling time of two hours. During that visit she takes toys for the children and plays with them, modelling discipline and suggesting new ways to manage. She helps with letters and documents. She encourages physical contact, hugs, comforts, praises and listens to mother's worries.*

February. *Two daytime visits this month of two hours and two and a half hours respectively. In addition the volunteer babysits on two evenings for two hours on each occasion. She plays with the children, washes up and shares cooking skills with the mother. She hugs and praises. The babysitting gives the parents a much needed chance to go out together. The volunteer also rings the mother for a chat three times.*
March. *Three visits of approximately two hours. The volunteer models discipline, shares cooking skills and plays with and reads to the children (one visit). She also takes the family out to tea and takes the children to the park.*

Mothers aged fourteen to seventeen years old made up five per cent of the participants in Home-Start schemes. Most had a background of having been in public care themselves and few had experienced stable backgrounds with parents on hand to support them. Consequently, they were lacking in the basic skills of budgeting, cooking and child care. Some were isolated and lacking in self-esteem, some suffered from violent partners. Volunteers gave two to five hours a week to the teenage mothers and helped in a variety of ways, including giving advice on breast feeding, showing how to give and receive affection, how to budget, demonstrating verbal communication with the baby, participating in cooking together, and introducing them to a young mothers' group. A typical example from *Family Album*:

Hayley and her family live in a warm and welcoming home on the edge of the town where she was born and brought up. She has twin boys of twenty months and a daughter of eight months. Her partner works locally but is poorly paid. Until recently they lived in a sub-standard damp flat with mould on the walls and blocked drains. The baby had been admitted to hospital several times, failing to gain weight and suffering from eczema and asthma, and Hayley was anxious about her. As tests did not initially show a medical cause, it was suggested by professionals that Hayley was not feeding her properly, adding to her stress. However, it has

*now been discovered that the baby has a milk allergy, the cause of
her failure to thrive...*

*A volunteer has visited Hayley and her family regularly since
the twins were born, at least once a week, sometimes more, and
has been alongside Hayley through many difficult times. Hayley
goes with her children to the Home-Start Group each week, where
she spends time with other young parents while the children are
looked after in a crèche. This gives her a breathing space when
she can spend time with her peers, and her children can spend
time in a stimulating environment. Most importantly, there is
someone who will listen, and who will believe in her.*

The question must be asked, does it work? Do all the
hours of visiting, all the hard work, all the taking out, all
the time spent playing with the children, have any
beneficial effect?

Willem Van der Eyken undertook an independent
four-year evaluation of Home-Start schemes. He devised
various measures of 'change' and used different
professionals to make judgments about what happened to
the families. The overall results were that, having been
visited by volunteers, 66 per cent of families showed
'considerable change' for the better, 26.9 per cent 'some
change' and 7.1 per cent 'no change'. The changes were
improvements in provision, such as the family being re-
housed into suitable accommodation or the children
joining a nursery school, relationship changes with improved functioning between parents and children, and
personal changes such as mothers becoming more self-
confident. Moreover, nearly all the children, including
those initially deemed as 'at risk', did not enter public
care but stayed with their families.

Perhaps, however, the most important judges are not
academic researchers or outside professionals but the
mothers themselves. What did they think? Families
followed up in the 1993 study by Shinman reported
that what they had wanted most was a friend, help with
the children, and to be listened to. With this in mind,

72 per cent expressed themselves as 'very satisfied' and few voiced dissatisfaction with the work of Head-Start. Some mothers specified particular achievements like gaining understanding of children, learning to cope, winning control over circumstances, and breaking out of isolation. One said that the volunteers 'saved the family from splitting up'. The strongest indicator that the schemes were worthwhile was that, after three months, ten mothers opted to take on training courses so as to become volunteers themselves.

Not just the professionals

One theme of this book is that a major approach to juvenile crime should be to prevent delinquency by strengthening vulnerable families. Clearly, many highly trained pro-fessionals—the police, probation officers, social workers, health visitors, psychologists and psychiatrists—play vital roles in the prevention, apprehension, treatment and punishment of juvenile delinquency. But this does not mean that ordinary citizens cannot be involved.

For a start, those who live in areas subject to much crime can initiate and be committee members of local voluntary bodies which employ expert staff to run day care centres, nursery schools, family centres and so on. More, a lesson to be drawn from the projects described in these chapters is that ordinary non- professionals can play a direct part in helping other families. In the Walcot Family Centre, it was volunteers who ran Neighbourhood Care Volunteers. In Newpin and Home-Start, the agencies depended largely upon volunteers who had no professional qualifications. In the next chapter, it will be seen that local parents and residents can play an important part in youth activities.

It is not being argued that the unqualified can adopt the Oregon approach and be like Gerald Patterson—that kind of therapy does have to be left to the professionals. But 'unqualified' people often have skills and qualities which can be of use to families in need. Moreover, the residents of the areas where the projects tend to be set up may well have characteristics lacking in the professionals who commute in and out. They often know the area very well, know its deficiencies: its lack of safe playspace, the poor bus service, the rip-off high food prices, the fear of local gangs and other factors which put pressure on young families. And they know its strengths: the stable members of the community, the potential volunteers, the teenagers who can help at the clubs, the buildings which can be utilized. Further, such residents often come from the same backgrounds as the vulnerable families: they too have lived in the council tenements, attended the same schools, drunk in the same pubs, worshipped in the same churches, supported the same football teams. Not least, they may have been through similar experiences to the families who approach family centres, Newpin, Home-Start and similar agencies. Some will have faced lone parenthood, unemployment, poverty, isolation, racism, perhaps delinquency. They can stand in the shoes of the people who now seek help.

Local knowledge, similar backgrounds and experiences are advantages which some local residents can bring to their roles as volunteers, as sessional staff, even as full-time staff in projects which reach out to parents finding it difficult to cope with their children. But these advantages on their own are not sufficient. Having worked for eighteen years in two community projects which relied heavily on local involvement, I can identify three qualities which make for the most effective participants:

Empathy or warmth

Volunteers, sessional workers, local staff—I'll call them participants—must be in sympathy with the users of the projects. This may seem an obvious point but there are sometimes participants who are prejudiced against certain types of users, who have grown embittered or disillusioned, who tire of the demands of users, who hold the old Poor Law attitude: 'They don't deserve to be helped.' Instead, participants require a genuine concern for others which is expressed in understanding, acceptance, humour and compassion. This is not to say that they are weak, can be walked over and manipulated, but that they can be firm without being nasty, strong without being rejecting.

Practicality

I am not a practical person. When I changed a light fitting in the kitchen, the outcome was that all the lights in our flat went on and off with the kitchen switch. One of my worst moments was when, while I was showing a film to a crowded junior youth club, the film shot out of the projector and I could not get it back in. As the kids howled at losing Spiderman halfway up a skyscraper, I had to call upon my much more practical colleague. At least I can tell corny jokes and that entertained the kids while he put the film back in.

In contrast, I've noticed neighbours who have practical abilities—the knack of starting cars, mending washing machines, wielding a paint brush. Being practical is not enough but it can be a tool which can be used on behalf of others. I think of a lone mother with a low sense of her own abilities who constantly came to our door in a state of depression: yet she proved ace at arts and crafts work and, once introduced into the junior youth club, soon had crowds of children around her as she showed them how to make models, paint pictures, construct games: her skills became the basis for her relationships with the youngsters and, in so doing, she did much to improve her own self-image.

A friend of mine went in every day to help a man who was devastated when his wife left, leaving him with three children. She helped him clean the house, taught him to cook, looked after the little ones until he could cope on his own. By this time he had built a trust in her which then allowed him to share some of his personal fears and problems with which he needed advice. Again, a local voluntary youth leader used his ability to mend bikes to strike up a friendship with a delinquent boy who was finding it difficult to fit into the youth club.

Endurance

Local projects rarely go from success to success. Family centres, nurseries, youth clubs, organizations like Newpin and Home-Start go in cycles of ups and downs. Their successes are emphasized in these chapters but it must also be said that they descend into the troughs when a lack of money threatens their continuance, when committee members argue and resign, when participants come out of a heavy evening and find their car smashed up, when users become hypercritical of the helpers. It is during these times that the real worth of participants is proved by their endurance. The ones of most use to projects are those who stay when others leave, who have stickability as much as ability. Often volunteers who start enthusiastically like a rush of wind, full of ideas of what they will do, are the first to leave. Those who join with a commitment combined with a readiness to listen and learn are usually the ones who survive and who become more reliable and more valuable than the very bricks of the building.

Having identified these three qualities, I read the book *Called To Action* by Fran Beckett of the Shaftesbury Society. It is addressed mainly to church members who want to help their neighbours, either through projects based within their churches or by joining outside agencies. She asks, 'What personal strengths are necessary in order to be effective in building bridges of relationships and care into the community?' Amongst the desirable qualities she lists is practical skills—identical with my observation. She then adds two others which, I reckon, are close to what I called empathy and endurance but which she calls sensitivity and reliability. She explains them as follows.

Sensitivity to others is a strength to be sought after and treasured. It means a growing ability to understand something of another person's situation and pain. The capacity to identify in such a way as to stand alongside, offering support when it's needed, and standing back when it's appropriate. Not superimposing upon others one's own feelings or responses from a similar situation but treating them as individuals, very special individuals. Feeling with them but not getting so sucked in that the boundaries between what is their perception and what is the helper's become unrecognizable.

Reliability. Part of our human frailty includes making rash commitments or promises that we never intend to keep, letting others down as a result. Disappointment is a common human experience. We all know at first hand how devastating it can be to be let down by someone else. A truth that God wants us to grasp is that his love is totally and eternally reliable. He is utterly consistent and not swayed by irrational whims or moods. Promises that He makes He keeps. For the ordinary person in the street that concept remains rather remote and meaningless if it is read about but not experienced. That is where the Church, and in particular individual Christians, come in. Wisdom in the nature of commitments made which leads to them being honoured, can actually make God's love more real for others.

Beckett is addressing church people but her ideal qualities are also needed by other volunteers. Practical skills, empathy or sensitivity, endurance or reliability, are essential for participants. When they are found in residents who have the additional advantages of local knowledge and experiences, they can make for very effective volunteers and members as the agencies described in these chapters have proved. But their effectiveness can still be improved by training, whether it be within the agencies or away on residential courses. At these, parents who are involved in supporting other parents can learn how to listen more effectively, how to offer advice, how to act with users to negotiate with statutory bodies for better services or increased benefits. And so on.

Further, all participants can be strengthened by regular meetings in which tactics and strategies are worked out and evaluated and at which tricky issues can be debated. Some such issues I have come across are: how to react if a mother, in confidence, reveals that she suspects that her partner is sexually abusing her child, how to respond if a poverty-stricken parent asks for a loan, what to do if one participant claims that another is stealing from the project? Projects have to develop guidelines covering such matters and they are best dealt with by the whole team.

At times, a local resident goes on to become a full-time staff member, as happened at the Walcot Family Centre. Their background and skills usually equip them well for leadership. But the aim is not to turn all local and able residents into full-time staff, for that would be neither possible nor desirable. Local projects appear to thrive best when they have a small number of full-time leaders backed by capable part-timers and volunteers whose strengths have been improved by training. The government's former health minister, Virginia Bottomley, said in 1993,

Bringing up children is difficult at the best of times. For some people, in tough circumstances, it becomes overwhelming. Children need protection and parents need encouragement and confidence... Parenthood is not a sprint. It is a marathon and it is not easy. It has to be shared with the local community, with neighbours and above all with families.

A main argument of this book is that much of this encouragement and sharing can come from ordinary but able citizens who are the backbone of local community associations, day care centres, family centres, Home-Start schemes, projects like Newpin and many others. In so doing they can help vulnerable families both to stay together and also to achieve the quality of child-rearing which enables their children to grow up in ways which are not delinquent. I hope this book will encourage more citizens to initiate and to volunteer to be involved in such ventures.

NINE

Something for Youngsters—Youth Work

The foundations of child development are laid down in the pre-school years and hence it has been argued that services to support parents in bringing up young children are the best means of preventing delinquency. But this does not mean that nothing can be done at later ages. Consider children at the primary or junior school stage. West, in *Delinquency: Its Roots, Careers and Prospects* (1982), found that 44 per cent of delinquent youngsters gave some hint of their future by being noted as 'troublesome' at school. To repeat an earlier point, other boys (and they are mainly boys, not girls) recorded as troublesome did not become delinquent so it would be counter-productive to isolate and treat them all as future law-breakers. None the less, it can still be concluded that this age group as a whole could well benefit from constructive youth programmes.

Of course, the peak age for actually committing delinquent acts comes later in the teenage years so here too there is scope for intervention. As youngsters grow older, so they become more independent of their parents. It follows that youth services, while not excluding parents, will concentrate more and more on helping young people outside their homes.

Once more, it must be said that statutory bodies have

far more influence on children than voluntary ones. After all, the children do spend a considerable part of their year in school. Further, local authorities have accepted much responsibility for promoting youth services. Beyond doubt, the statutory youth service must take credit for stimulating innovative services, for insisting on the value of training, for promoting activities which are more sensitive to the needs of minority ethnic groups, and for encouraging youth groups which are of interest to and relevant to girls. But there is still scope for contributions by voluntary bodies, and not just the large national societies, but churches, community groups and other small associations of local people. The scope exists because sometimes young people feel that school is too much a part of the 'establishment' and react by disruptive behaviour or truanting. It may therefore be better to offer help and activities provided outside the statutory sector. And the scope exists because often local authorities are having to cut back on their youth provision.

For instance, the London borough of Hackney has maintained a number of youth centres of good reputation. One is Colvestone Youth Centre in an area characterized by much crime and drugs. The centre is noted for its extensive sports and arts programmes, its boxing gym, weight training, kung-fu instruction, photography club, table tennis and many other outlets for young people. It has existed for forty years and its volunteer helpers include numbers of adults who came through the centre in their young days. Unfortunately, facing a financial crisis, the local authority has had to reduce staff hours by 80 per cent at Colvestone and other youth centres. Similar cutbacks have occurred all over Britain for youth work, unlike school, is a discretionary not a mandatory service and so, in times of economic restraint, is a prime target for expenditure cuts. Michael Eastman travels all over Britain in his work with the Frontier Youth Trust and, noting the decline, wrote,

The brave new world of our Government-inspired 'Contract Culture' hasn't helped. The Youth Service as a voluntary/statutory partnership has been dismantled with hardly a murmur. Occasionally we read in the press about the irony of closing a youth centre and a consequent increase of car crime and shoplifting. The police are left to hold the line and tell the story in vain. The language of the market with 'inputs', 'outputs' and 'performance indicators' has entered our vocabulary. As local authorities become contractors for, rather than providers of, services, the ethos governing publicly funded provision changes. This wears off on all of us. The young feel increasingly disenfranchised. Along with this change in the delivery of services has come substantial cuts in the resources available. The numbers of paid professionally-trained youth workers has declined from 5,000 to 3,000 on some estimates.

The sad decline of statutory youth work makes the contribution of voluntary projects all the more important. Of course, the voluntary clubs themselves often rely upon grants from local authorities. But they can seek other sources. Moreover, they sometimes have one distinct advantage. Their members often live in the areas of greatest social need and so are on the spot to offer help.

What kind of services can they contribute? At the risk of over-simplification, youth services for youngsters can be divided into two kinds—what I call ordinary youth clubs, open to a wide band of residents; and specialized ones, which attempt to cater for young people with more intense problems. After giving examples of both these approaches, I shall then argue that they should not be cut off from the rest of the community. I shall conclude by identifying the features which make for sound youth work.

Ordinary youth clubs

After several years in academic life, I returned to what is sometimes called 'field work'. I'm not sure if 'field work' is an appropriate term, for I operated in an urban council estate in the south-west of England. As the sole employee of a new and small project, I started by knocking on doors and asking residents what they thought was needed in their district. One woman replied that she needed a rich bloke of about forty. As I opened another gate, an upstairs window flew open and a voice screamed, 'If you're the bleedin' welfare, clear off.' At another, a dog's teeth grasped the seat of my trousers as I leapt over the fence. Generally, however, people were pleasantly surprised that their views were being sought and often I was invited in for a cup of tea and a chat. They told me about the noise in the streets, the motor bikes roaring up and down, the vandalism, youngsters shouting late at night, kids playing football in the road so that windows got broken. Their common request was for me to find the youngsters something to do.

I wanted to know also what the youngsters felt and what they wanted. In the evenings, I began to dawdle in the streets and gradually got into conversations with them. At times I felt threatened as they surrounded me by a lamp post and turned the tables by questioning me.

'You've been talking to my mum, ain't yer?'

'Are you a probation officer? I'm on probation.'

'What are you doing here?'

I tried to explain about the project and that I wanted their opinions. They told me that there was nowhere to go and nothing to do. It was all 'boring'. And they were fed up with the adults, including their parents, always grumbling at them. After more conversations in the street, a number called at our house and asked if I would start a youth club. I replied that I would not start a club but that we could do it together. We called a meeting and about twenty youngsters crowded into our front room. It was agreed to go ahead, a committee was elected with a twenty-year-old, Dave Wiles, as chairperson. Dave's involvement proved crucial. He had a delinquent record, was on probation for drugs offences and had a reputation as a hard man. But Dave had recently undergone a dramatic conversion to Christianity and now wanted to put something back into the community—hence his interest in the youth club. He had been feared and was now respected in the community. He could communicate with local teenagers far better than me. Further, the way he accepted me, and our growing friendship, eased my relationships with them.

The major initial problem was to find somewhere to hold the club. The schools were not open to the community in the evenings. The churches were wary of the kind of teenagers I wanted to bring in. We started to meet in our house although it was far too small. Then we came across three old pre-fabs. They were leased by an artist but, as he was going through a financial crisis, he was prepared to rent out one to us for the club. It had no heating save an impossible-to-light boiler but it had space. We were in.

The club work expanded. Clubs for seniors, clubs for juniors, a club for girls only. The expansion was possible for two reasons. One was the involvement of a number of parents with the junior activities. The other was the recognition by church leaders that the youth club members would not wreck their halls: a window might get broken, but the teenagers did not, as they had imagined, tear around on motor bikes inside the hall and did not attack the church cleaner. Before long, the church leaders were asking me to run clubs for them.

What did the clubs do? Basically they gave the youngsters a place where they could spend much of their leisure time. The activities inside the halls were nothing special—table tennis on a battered table which some of the kids found on a dump, pool on a table which we had to carry from place to place, darts, music, a café. But before there had been nothing and it was dry and safe. Certainly, the parents expressed appreciation that they knew where their children were going.

The clubs were not just entertainment. They were also something of a counter to delinquency. I was told how some juvenile offenders attributed their waywardness to boredom: the boredom of hanging about on the streets for hours with little to do. Some of the youngsters who joined our clubs told me how they would go shoplifting for the excitement of outwitting the store detectives, how they got a kick out of crashing the vehicles which work-men left overnight on building sites, and how they enjoyed talking about their successes in housebreaking. At least, the clubs with their associated discos and sports matches gave them other and enjoyable outlets. It is not argued that boredom is the root cause of delinquency: obviously most bored young people do not commit offences. But it is a contributory cause and, for vulnerable youngsters, the clubs provided an alternative means of meeting others in activities which were not considered soft or square. Moreover, in the clubs they mixed with peers who were not delinquent and with some adults who were stable figures in the community.

Later Dave Wiles joined the project as a full-time worker. Eventually, with the aid of much local fund-raising, a permanent building was obtained. The youth activities multiplied even more rapidly to include before-school and lunch-time clubs. The clubs were well attended and still continue. Looking back, I see the following factors as underpinning the success of such clubs:

Planning

The club's activities must be planned. If leaders and helpers turn up at the last minute and just unlock the doors, then they will find, especially with juniors, that interest and enthusiasm flags. The leaders should be there beforehand both to get the equipment out and to welcome members as they come through the door. Further, they should have planned the programme for a whole term so that members know and can look forward to the snooker competition, the daft olympics night, the one-legged disco competition, the visit from another youth club, darts versus the parents' team, or whatever.

Objectives

It is essential to have an objective: something which the club is working towards. One night, at our senior club, a boy came in all steamed up about the low wages a paraplegic friend of his was receiving in a sheltered workshop. After discussions within the club and with his friend, it was agreed that the club would raise the money to buy him a washing machine specially adapted for his use. Following various fund-raising efforts the objective was reached and the washing machine presented to and used by the friend. The club members had discovered that, for all their own disadvantages, they too could help others. Moreover, the resulting publicity in the press, gave them (and other residents) a more positive image of the young people on the estate. Not least, the paraplegic youngster became a regular member of the club as well.

Seasons

Clubs must close some time. No, I'm not joking. There must be periods when the doors are shut. Non-stop club activity can become boring as well. In the summer evenings, we found it best to close the clubs and to organize some events outside. Fortunately, we were near a patch of common land that gave scope for cricket, football, races etc in the open air. Once the project obtained a minibus, it was possible to arrange a summer programme of trips to swimming, boating, skating, barbecues at a friend's farm. After a few weeks outside, club members looked forward to being indoors again.

Club holidays

Clubs usually close altogether for a month or so in the summer and it is a great advantage if the club season ends with a club holiday. Dave, the volunteers and myself organized various kinds of holidays for the different age groups. One was under canvas, another in a large country house, a third at Butlin's.

The holidays can have hairy moments. A college principal gave us permission to camp in the grounds of his teachers' training college where we enjoyed all its facilities—swimming pool, gym, full-size snooker tables. Unfortunately, some of the staff did not share the principal's enthusiasm for opening up the college, were not co-operative, and, at one point, accused the campers of breaking into the bar. The Butlin's holiday was a great success except for the aftermath: on the return trip, a teenage girl was suddenly sick in the minibus so that her vomit shot across the front windscreen, nearly causing a crash as I braked hard; we had to clear everything out in order to clean the inside. On our return home, some parents heard that their sixteen-year-old daughter had had sex with one of our boys at the camp and angrily told me that I was irresponsible for allowing such behaviour. At times like that I felt like giving up. But almost as soon as we were back, the youngsters were saying how brilliant it had been and were planning for next year. Club holidays not only give time away for youngsters who probably otherwise would not go, they also help mould members into a cohesive unit.

Clubs do not suit all youngsters. Some can be unduly aggressive or withdrawn in large groups of thirty or more. The more demanding and difficult youngsters can often be best helped within small groups. Dave Wiles and I perceived this need on the estate and gradually developed activities for smaller numbers. We deliberately drew in delinquent teenagers or those on the fringes of delinquency yet, not wishing the groups to be stigmatized as for 'the bad 'uns', we balanced the membership with others. Drawing in the former was never a problem, for a few—noticed for their truancy, court appearances or disruptive behaviour—were seeking our company. Simultaneously we were getting close to other youngsters who dropped in for a bowl of soup at lunch-time or a cup of coffee in the evening.

We began to take them out in groups of about six with a focus on a particular activity which appealed to them. We did table tennis at the sports centre, went regularly to speedway racing, had a Saturday trip to a professional football match, did a course in trampolining. and, most terrifying, did parascending which involves dangling on a parachute drawn along by a Range Rover. Usually we would return to our house and, over a bag of chips, would discuss the events of the day and then get into conversation about such matters as the dangers of truancy, what it was like not having a dad at home, the risks attached to stealing, the injustice of a world in which the privileged had so much and the deprived so little. One day we discussed the reactions of some of the group who had responded aggressively to a doorman who would not let them into a bingo hall. We made a video about shoplifting, with Dave and me playing the parts of the delinquents and the youngsters those of magistrates, parents, police and probation officers. Hopefully they gained some appreciation of making decisions from the officials' point of view.

Groups are not always happy experiences. Rivalries can break out, members can be scapegoated. But overall they are a means of drawing needy young people into friendship circles which both entertain them and also give them some understanding of their own behaviour. Delinquency did not stop on the estate, but the combined outcomes of the clubs and groups did appear to reduce the number of juvenile court appearances.

Specialized youth work

Some years ago, the Newcastle-upon-Tyne YMCA decided that its well-equipped city centre premises were being under-used . Youngsters with money tended to buy their leisure at commercial discos, clubs and bars, while those without money could not afford to travel from the estates into town. Its managing committee then made the important decision to let out its central premises to an educational institution and to use the rent as a steady income towards projects which would reach out to vulnerable young people. In particular, two new projects were aimed to serve those aged fifteen to twenty-five years old residing in areas of social deprivation.

The Walker Project

The Walker Project is set within an estate and its premises are open to youngsters just to drop in. The kind of problems they bring tend to be about difficulties in finding accommodation, and understanding and using the benefits provided by the Department of Social Security. The project workers give advice on these matters and also support those who have fallen foul of the police and the courts. Their friendship continues even if the youngsters are committed to prison, for they later need help with returning to and settling into the neighbourhood again. Others have come for counselling about emotional rejections they have faced, about their depression after years of unemployment, and the state of their physical health.

But not all young people will walk into an agency. The two project workers and three part-time staff therefore spend much time outside the building, striking up conversations and entering into street activities. Once trusted, they invite young residents to make use of the project's premises and services. From these contacts, a number of groups have been formed. The Young Women's Group arose from a request from the eighteen-to twenty-five-year-olds who were hanging about the streets. With the project worker, they planned a pro- gramme of activities divided into six-week blocks so that progress could be reviewed at the end of each block. They went ten-pin bowling and swimming; had sessions on diet and nutrition; enjoyed cookery workshops; and a nurse from the local family planning clinic ran sessions on contraception and women's health. Once the group finished, its members continued to call at the project and to support each other. Meanwhile, the project workers are initiating another women's group.

A Young Men's Group came into being in similar fashion. It ran a number of outside activities, often of a sporting or musical nature, which allowed the members to gell into a circle able to discuss issues of importance. They mulled over what was acceptable and unacceptable behaviour in the group and outside, they discussed what kind of male image people like them needed to have about themselves, they considered what were their responsibilities in regard to safe sex and fatherhood, they debated the rights and wrongs of crime. Gradually, the group reached the stage where it could set down its own rules of behaviour and plan its own programme.

These groups are just two examples. In any one month, the Walker Project contacts 180–200 local young people. With drugs a growing problem, the project staff also give out information about what drugs do to human chemistry and behaviour and try to cultivate knowledge so that people can make informed decisions in an atmosphere in which it becomes acceptable to say 'no'.

Project 10

Project 10, also with two full-time staff and three sessional workers, is based in a two-bedroomed flat in a multi-storey block. The block is one of ten high-rise flats in Cruddas Park which is a part of West City, a ward characterized by much unemployment and a concen-tration of single young people. Many of the latter face problems of poverty, coping alone, unemployment, losing their tenancies and then homelessness.

The staff try to visit new tenants as soon as they move into the flats. They present them with a starter pack consisting of toiletries, washing-up liquid, light bulbs and so on, and tell them what the project is about. They hear that the project's flat is open two afternoons a week for drop-in sessions where advice on welfare rights benefits, HIV and AIDS, budgeting, education and careers is given. Many young people in Cruddas Park face difficulties in obtaining such essential items as fridges, cookers, fires and warm clothes, so the project has collected a stock of these for distribution at modest prices. These initial contacts over practical matters sometimes lead on to more in-depth counselling for those who have come with difficulties about sexual abuse, sexual behaviour, pregnancy, abortions, custody of children, bereavements, drug taking and criminal behaviour. Often the staff become resourceful friends (see Chapter 10) who are there when needed and who accompany young people to meetings with statutory departments or to court. The female project worker was on hand to rush a user to hospital, where she had the thrill of staying with her while her baby was born.

Here too the individual contacts have allowed the formation of groups. The Food Group involved a community dietician teaching eight teenagers how to cook and about what constituted healthy eating. Cooking and eating together encouraged a sense of cooperation and the group then produced a cookbook entitled *More Nosh Less Dosh*. One Step Ahead was a group established to help educate young people about the problems of leaving home. The Art Project included a two-day photo-montage workshop and led to participants holding an exhibition of their work. Not least, in 1993 project staff took a group to Spain for a holiday. The following year they placed the responsibility in the hands of three of the previous holiday-makers. They were given some training in fund-raising, dealing with conflict within the group, and in selecting the new party. The three organizers undertook the fund-raising and then brought together the ones who were selected in order to discuss the programme, to understand the Spanish currency and to learn some basic Spanish. Despite some setbacks, the eventual holiday was a great success. For most of the group it was their first time abroad. For the three organizers, it was an achievement of which they could feel proud.

Who are the young people served by Project 10? 42 per cent have been in public care and hence have not experienced stable family backgrounds. 67 per cent have been homeless at some stage. All have very low incomes. A typical example is one young person whose Giro benefit amounts to £36.16 per week from which rent, heat, light, clothes and food have to be paid. Little, if any, is left for leisure or travel costs. Clearly, Project 10 is reaching out to vulnerable young people, vulnerable in that both their past upbringing and their present deprivations could push them into delinquency.

The Walker and Project 10 schemes are small but important examples of detached youth work, that is, of agencies whose staff are not located in offices or project buildings but who spend most of their time on the streets or in pubs or discos where contact can more easily be made with young people who may be alienated from mainstream society. Michael Eastman, reflecting upon his thirty years' experience in youth work, concludes that the young people who are 'on the edge, shut out and held down in our society' require three provisions from the youth services, as follows:

♦ safe places in which they can feel at home, where they are not threatened by authority, not condemned by the affluent, not controlled by the powerful;

♦ :a street presence whereby committed staff meet young people on their own ground, in places with which they feel familiar;

♦ crisis accommodation so that help is at hand at the times of desperation when they are kicked out, arrested, depressed, tempted to steal or take drugs. Youth projects which make these provisions surely hold back some young people on the threshold of delinquency and so enable them to live more safe, secure and satisfying lives.

Undoubtedly, projects of this kind require staff with experience, skills and qualities of toughness and endurance. As with the nursery schools, it is not suggested that the average residents of the inner cities and council estates (or anywhere else) should attempt the task. However, these residents as members of local bodies could initiate and manage such projects.

The costs? In 1993–94, the Walker Project cost £65,183 and Project 10 £52,883, the main expenditure going on salaries. In these cases, the projects raised some of their own money, with the YMCA contributing the rest. Similarly, local committees could work in conjunction with local authority housing departments, who might well supply premises at low cost, and with charitable trusts for other expenses. Even in these days of cut-backs, some new ventures are still getting off the ground.

Youth and community

Ordinary youth clubs and specialized youth approaches do not have to be, and should not be, cut off from other community activities. My experience leads me to give three reasons why young people are best served by youth services which fit into a framework of other neighbourhood activities.

First, young people, as much as older ones, have a need to belong to and to identify with the social and geographical whole which is usually called the community. If they are alienated from that community then they are more likely to steal from and vandalize it. If they feel a part of it, they are more likely to protect it and to promote its well-being.

Second, there is danger that in treating young people as an entity quite different from their environment, youth services may actually intensify the split between them and their families. Of course, adolescence is a period when young people do grow—and need to grow—more independent of their parents. Indeed, youth services may well be one means in which they do learn about independence in a safe setting. Teenagers sometimes need to talk to adults outside their immediate family and youth leaders can properly act in this role. But this growth to independence is best done in conjunction with parents.

I recall some families taking me aside and explaining that they felt left out when the clubs took their children on holidays. Subsequently, our club arranged some family holidays and also arranged the occasional parent night at the youth club. If parents know what goes on inside the local youth services, then they are less likely to have suspicions about them. If they know and trust the youth leaders then they are less likely to see them as a threat, even as rival parental figures. Indeed, sometimes in times of stress and conflict, parents and young people need someone to mediate between them, and that role can be taken on by a youth leader who is known to and respected by both sides. Youth services are of most use to parents and young people when they are regarded as a part of the local community, not an agency quite distinct from it.

Third, a variety of interlocking facilities can enable growing youngsters to proceed from one to another with little stress and with a sense that they are part of a community. At best, they can move through playgroups, junior and senior clubs, sporting teams and into those social activities which are for adults. In this way, young people can have separate activities without feeling separated from the adult life of the neighbourhood. A range of community facilities may be supplied by one strong community association or church, or it may be the accumulation of a variety of independent agencies in the same neighbourhood. Here are examples of each type:

Holme Christian Care Centre

Holme United Reformed Church on the large council estate of Holmewood in Bradford undertakes youth club work and has close links with local schools. But, far more than that, the church, under the leadership of the Rev. Alan Evans and Andy Dolton, has pioneered the Holme Christian Care Centre, which is an attempt to express Christian values in practical ways. A small mums and tots group has expanded into a large play centre attended by around 200 pre-school children each week.

In an area with much unemployment, the centre has two full-time workers who run a daily drop-in centre where unemployed people can find friendship, help and advice. The staff can also link them with local employers so that long-term unemployed residents have found jobs. But often the job hunt requires candidates needing new skills so the centre provides training in typing, word processing, desktop publishing and GCSEs. A weekly Gateway Club provides educational and social activities for thirty young people with special needs. Two adults with such needs are part of a team which improves pensioners' gardens. Luncheon clubs for elderly people, a visiting scheme to the housebound and a neighbourhood advice centre, which specializes in welfare benefits and debt counselling, complete the comprehensive programme which now employs thirty full-time staff and involves many volunteers. Where does the money come from? From giving by church members, by support from local firms, from grants from the local authority, and £150,000 from the government's City Challenge Initiative.

Local groups in Easterhouse

In the Rogerfield district of Easterhouse—an estate even larger than Holmewood—there is an absence of buildings which can be used for community activities. Yet a number of local groups have been established. A tenants' association provides frequent advice for members and has initiated some clubs for children. FARE (Family Action In Rogerfield and Easterhouse) is a local project whose committee is elected by residents. It runs numerous youth clubs, at lunch-times and evenings, within the local schools. It uses, free of charge, the small Salvation Army hall for other children's activities; its minibus has proved invaluable for taking families to swimming, ten-pin bowling and out to parks. In the summer, FARE arranges for about 150 residents to have holidays, ranging from adventure-style ventures for teenagers to camping for younger children and family holidays, at a residential centre belonging to the St George's and St Peter's Community Association. This association, as mentioned in a previous chapter, maintains an excellent day care facility and also a visiting scheme to the elderly.

During the holiday weeks, local parents, with the aid of a small grant from the council, run a playscheme for junior children. Based at one of the schools, this scheme has, for many years, enabled those children to enjoy craft, music and games in a safe environment. On an estate with no major banks and only one branch of the TSB to serve a large population, low interest credit has been hard to obtain, with the result that loan sharks have flourished. In response, eighteen residents in this district came together and undertook training which enabled them to found the North Easterhouse Credit Union. Simultaneously another credit union was established using St George's and St Peter's as a base. The outcome has been the availability of legal, low-credit loans for the whole district. Lastly, a food co-op came into being with members using FARE's minibus to purchase food from cash and carrys and markets and then selling at low cost bread, milk, toilet rolls, tinned food, fruit and vegetables more cheaply than from local shops and vans. Unfortunately, a series of break-ins forced the closure of the co-op, although it hopes to start again.

These two examples are not unique. The Community Development Foundation estimates that two-and-a-half million people participate in local community groups, nearly all on budgets of under £10,000 a year, many in areas of high social deprivation. These community activities are important for all residents but, in the context of this book, have a particular relevance to youngsters who may be drawn into delinquency.

As we have seen, local youth clubs are of direct help to them during their school-age years. When of employable age, they can benefit from the kind of on-the-spot job services at Holmewood. When setting up their own homes, they can make use of the low credit and cheap food in credit unions and food co-ops. As young parents, their children can be stimulated by attendance at day care centres. In short, neighbourhood services can support young people at critical stages of human development. Simultaneously, local projects for residents with special needs, whether young or old, provide opportunities for young people to volunteer to serve others.

Thus a neighbourhood with a variety of services not only ensures leisure and friendship activities for the young but also can involve them in projects which uphold the values of sharing, co-operation and responsibility—in the long run, the surest counter to crime.

It must be said that many areas most in need of extensive community projects do not possess them. Further, even where they do exist, they are not always models of harmony and sometimes conflict breaks out between the generations over access to local facilities. Not least, the funding problems of small, independent projects means that some do not endure. None the less, the research evidence, as reviewed by Marjorie Mayo in *Community and Caring*, suggests that community projects do make for socially stronger neighbourhoods which, in turn, are of much help to young residents.

Right features for youth services

Just as community projects in general do not always run smoothly, so local youth services in particular often hit difficulties. For instance, Project 10 had a serious problem when some of its regular users became apathetic about activities and at the same time became hostile towards any newcomers who wanted to join. The senior youth club which Dave Wiles and I initiated went through a shaky patch with feuds and fighting between different cliques resulting in some regulars deciding to leave. There are times when funds are scarce, youngsters become hyper-critical, parents blame leaders for lack of control, and exhausted volunteers or staff give up. None the less, having had the privilege of seeing numerous youth activities all over Britain, I remain convinced of the value of youth work. My judgment is that the best youth projects, particularly those close to youngsters who are prone to delinquency, are characterized by two features in addition to being integrated with other local neigh-bourhood projects.

Responsible committees

Youth centres, clubs, groups should not just be left to the leaders. They require committees, preferably elected at annual general meetings by a wider membership, to which they are accountable. The committee should set policy, appoint staff (if any), and be responsible for finances. It should act as a liaison between the youth project and the rest of the community. It should ensure that the project maintains an equal opportunities policy and that it complies with local and national standards such as those set down in the Children Act 1989. The committee should encourage staff and volunteers to undertake training. This may entail attending courses run by training institutions which lead to formal qualifications or to in-service training.

FARE in Easterhouse, for instance, took nine of its volunteers, all but one unemployed parents, for a weekend on a Scottish island where an experienced trainer from outside formed them into small groups which identified the purposes of youth work, discussed relevant issues, such as dealing with disruptive members, and debated how best to involve the youngsters in decision-making. The trainer then set the groups the task of devising programmes and new games which were presented to the rest of the participants for their evaluation. They returned physically refreshed, with clearer thinking and new ideas.

Not least, the committee should be aware of what is happening within the clubs and so be able to offer support and guidance to club leaders. This might concern new tactics or strategies, for sometimes youth activities can get into a rut. At one time, FARE's committee advised its leaders to widen the scope of their work to include the pupils of more than one school. Another time, it perceived that it was not reaching enough girls and took steps to remedy its outreach. Perhaps most important, the committee needs to encourage the leaders during the hard times, when numbers fall away and when criticisms are being voiced. To give one example: a leader may give extra time and attention to a small number of youngsters who have appeared before the juvenile court: some local parents voice their opinion that these 'hooligans' do not deserve to be helped and that club resources should go to kids who behaved themselves. The role of the committee should be both to back the leaders and also to explain to the parents the aims and methods of the youth project.

Long-term commitment

I sometimes listen to clients of the social services who complain that their social workers are always changing. In like manner, young people are unsettled by frequent changes of staff and volunteers. The most successful youth projects, I reckon, are those where leaders make a commitment to stay several years.

It is not always easy to stay. Dave Wiles and I were later joined in the youth club work by a young woman with a middle-class accent which local kids immediately picked up to imitate. But she stuck it out, stayed for years and so won the respect and trust of residents. Some young people, especially those from unstable backgrounds, take a long time to form relationships and so it is essential to have staff who last. Further, it is over time that the leaders understand the local neighbourhood and its inhabitants. They identify the people who can become volunteers and the premises which can be used for clubs. Perhaps more importantly, they perceive the behaviour characteristics of the youngsters and know the moods, the words, the attitudes which indicate that something is wrong and extra help is required. Not least, it is over time that leaders understand both the negative and positive sides of young people.

As a former local authority social worker, I sometimes had to write reports on young people appearing before the courts. I met them for the first time when their delinquency was at its height and when all their negative behaviour was most obvious and, no doubt, these initial impressions were expressed in my words to the courts. But working and playing alongside young people over the years gives opportunities to see them in the good and the bad times, when they are at ease as well as when they are under stress, and thus it becomes possible to identify the strengths of their characters. If appearing in court with them, it is useful to be able to point out that they are not all bad. More, within the community, it is usually possible to give praise for their positive features and to encourage them to develop their strengths. There are many advantages of providing long-term services.

'Something for youngsters' comes in a variety of forms. There are large clubs with well equipped centres and several full-time staff, and there are those in small halls dependent upon volunteers. There are those which cater for a wide range of age groups who mostly live at home with their parents, and there are those which specialize in older young people who tend to live independently. There are those which have the benefit of being alongside a number of other community provisions, and there are those which struggle on almost alone. But all these types will be stronger if backed by enthusiastic and supportive committees and more effective if possessed of long-term leaders. They will be useful to many youngsters who are not prone to delinquency—and so they should be, for youth services want to reach all kinds of young people. But they can also be of particular help to those whose backgrounds, upbringing and behaviour do veer them towards illegal pursuits. The youth projects can help them by

◆ offering interesting legitimate pursuits which are an alternative to illegal ones;

◆ involving them in friendship groups which are not delinquent;

◆ giving advice and practical help for those facing the kind of depriving social conditions which make young people liable to delinquency;

◆ giving contact with adults who may offer friendship.

This last theme will be taken up in the next chapter.

TEN

Resourceful Friends— Befriending Young People

During the 1970s, statutory and voluntary bodies developed what was called Intermediate Treatment, IT for short. 'Intermediate' implied a means of help which was something between helping offenders just within their own families and taking them away into residential institutions.

The schemes were varied in kind. Some attempted to develop character by taking youngsters on adventure-type pursuits such as rock climbing and canoeing. Others focussed on specific offences like car theft and joy-riding: here the offenders were taught how to drive properly on private ground, as well as the basics of vehicle maintenance, with the intention that their criminal exploits would be cultivated towards legal ends so that they might eventually find jobs as mechanics and drivers. All the schemes also included individual and group counselling aimed at making the offenders face up to the effects of their crimes on others, the implications for their own futures if they committed further offences, and ways of avoiding future delinquency.

Intermediate Treatment has survived into the 1990s despite cuts in funding. NCH Action for Children (formerly the National Children's Home) has been a leading promoter of IT. Its policy officer, Sandy Ruxton, was quoted in the social work periodical *Community Care* in 1994, concerning this approach to character building:

This type of scheme was popular in the seventies but is less so now. A young offender may well have a positive experience halfway up a cliff and reflect on his or her behaviour, but whether its effects will be maintained when he or she gets home is another matter. There is a strong feeling that for schemes to work, they must operate in the young person's community.

Accordingly, schemes have been developed within the home neighbourhoods of young offenders. Typically they include activities which are intended to be an interesting alternative to delinquent exploits. Individual relationships between IT staff and the youngsters enable them to look at their particular problems and explore solutions; and group work contributes to a positive feeling amongst the members which becomes peer pressure to steer them away from crime. Research findings tend to show that not only is IT cheaper than custodial care but also that it is more effective.

Relationships

Intermediate Treatment schemes are usually run by professionally qualified staff who have the time to see the groups two to three times a week, are adept at group work, who have access to specialist resources—such as those necessary for car vehicle courses—and who sometimes can exercise authority delegated to them by the courts. It is not suggested here that members of churches, community associations and community groups can or should run IT. However, there is one element which can be exercised by them—within IT, staff make close relationships or friendships with young offenders as a means of exercising a positive influence on their values and behaviour. This medium can also be used by residents who are not qualified professionals.

Friendship is not quite the appropriate word, for this usually means a benevolent relationship between two persons in the same age-range. Here I am talking about a deliberately cultivated relationship between an older person and a younger one with the former bringing concern, stability, integrity and certain skills in order to help the latter. Of course, the older person may well enjoy and gain satisfaction from the friendship but the primary intention is less mutual benefit and more a concentration on the needs of the younger person. I call this *resourceful friendship*.

An example of a delinquent who profited from resourceful friendships is found in the autobiography of Tom O'Neill, *A Place Called Hope*. Tom came from a poverty-stricken and neglectful family and soon became a young criminal. Eventually he was removed from his family and sent to a remand home, then to an approved school. Discharged home in his teens, he was left with 'bitterness, loneliness and misery'. The experiences did him little good, for soon he was stealing again. However, on conviction, the magistrates placed him on probation with the condition that he should reside in a hostel run by the Salvation Army. The people in that hostel were to have an enormous influence on him. He wrote,

I will refer to the man in charge of that hostel as the Major, although when I first met him his rank in the Salvation Army was that of adjutant. He was promoted later. As far as this man is concerned, I consider rank to be unimportant. It was he himself who had such an impact on the lives of myself and others, not his status in the Salvation Army.

Perhaps even more significant for Tom was the Major's wife:

I will call her Auntie. She was a right old dragon at times, but it is rather strange that I use that term with affection. When Auntie was on the warpath everybody, and I mean everybody, gave her

right of way. But what a woman she was! A frail-looking woman, thin of face, grey hair tied with a bun at the back of the head, almost all covered by her Salvation Army bonnet. A great preacher who could hold any congregation spellbound. Bouncing with energy, her service for people seemed to be limitless. It didn't matter what time of the day or night she was called upon, she was always willing, always available, to do the best she could... There were a lot of young people she tried to help. Apart from the boys in the home, a large number of young people from the village used to go to the 'Army'—to the religious meetings, band practice, youth club and what have you. They all became her responsibility. 'I am your spiritual mother,' she used to say. She would talk to the kids for hours on end. If any one of them had a problem, she would take time out to talk to him individually and guide him through his difficulties. It sounds trite, but this was literally true; she always found time... eventually some of this willingness to help others rubbed off on me. I once spent many hours reading to and tending a retired hairdresser who had been paralysed by a stroke. I cannot pretend that the service I gave was of a high standard, but it was the desire to help others that really mattered. I hope that the atmosphere of the place and the attitudes and warmth of the people will permeate through the words that I write, so that the influence they had on my life and my future will become clear.

And there was Gran. Tough, hard Gran. Gran was a huge woman who walked with a peculiar gait, as if she had to drag one side of her body. She often seemed to be grinning from one side of her face only. She smiled fairly often, but more often she was very serious. She was responsible for the catering arrangements at the hostel... There were times, when we were peeling potatoes, or scrubbing the floor, or washing up, when we could talk to Gran. She didn't say an awful lot in return but seemed to be interested in what we had to say. When one of the boys was going through a rough period she wouldn't treat him gently or offer advice; she seemed to back-pedal with boys working in the kitchen and didn't push them as hard as she normally would. I once saw her weeping about one of the boys. She lived in a large bedroom on the premises, and rumour had it that she was quite well off financially, but she would not hesitate to send boys along to her bedroom to fetch something for her. This made them feel that, in spite of their murky pasts, they had come to a place where they were trusted... These people and many more like them, both at the hostel and afterwards, gave me a welcome and an acceptance I had never had before. Although none of them was a qualified social worker, they really cared.

At the hostel, Tom fell in love with a girl who worked there. After Tom completed his national service in the RAF, they married and he continues,

I settled down to normal married life. I worked in the coal mines and lived near to the hostel. I did a lot of spare-time work at the hostel and there were even occasions when my wife and I would sleep there so that the Major and his wife could have a holiday.

The Major and his wife were continually telling us that we should consider taking up residential child care work. They felt there was a great deal we could offer to deprived children.

In 1956, Tom and his wife did obtain a post in a children's home. They were still in the work in 1970 when the Major died. Tom recorded,

I attended his funeral, as I had his wife's two years earlier. As I watched his coffin being lowered gently into the grave, with his hat sitting proudly on top of it, I said a silent 'Thank you'. It took him a long time; it caused him a lot of heartache; it meant many long hours of work; but he eventually succeeded. He finally managed to make me believe in myself... he seemed to understand; more important, he cared.

Interestingly, Tom had a younger brother, Dennis, who was placed in a foster home where he was so cruelly treated that he died. As I have explained elsewhere, the scandal surrounding his death in 1945 was one of the factors which contributed to the passing of the Children Act of 1948. (See *The Evacuation*, Holman, 1995.) This Act led to the establishment of the very local authority children's departments with whom Tom was to spend his working life as a house-parent. So the two brothers represent the two extremes of how children, removed from their own homes, may be treated. The foster parents, Mr and Mrs Gough, who took in Dennis, used him for their own ends, as cheap labour for their farm and for gratification of Mr Gough's sadistic temper. What was it about the Major, his wife and their colleagues which made them, by contrast, such a power for good? It was not, as Tom points out, that they had special training or diplomas. Rather they possessed the following qualities.

Care

They genuinely cared for Tom. It was not a forced affection, not a front to impress others in order to win a grant or a contract: it was genuine care expressed in the sacrifice they were prepared to make for him and others. It was an unconditional affection offered, not to the easy-to-like, but to young delinquents who had been unable to fit into society at large.

Example

They led by example. The Major and his wife were far from perfect but generally they displayed qualities of concern, compassion, honesty and sheer goodness which Tom eventually took as a model for himself. The whole course of his life—and that of other youngsters—his behaviour, his beliefs, even his career, were shaped by what he saw and valued in them.

Skills

They brought skills. The Salvation Army couple may not have possessed a paper certificate to frame and display on the wall but they did possess attributes of leadership, of understanding, of communicating, of keeping control, of counselling. They were resourceful friends.

Their attitudes, skills and lifestyle were moulded into what is sometimes called the capacity to make relationships. They related to Tom and, in time, he responded with affection, help and loyalty, which they were able to accept.

Today there are still many Toms around. Research by the Institute of Criminology in Cambridge, which interviewed a large number of thirteen- to seventeen-year-olds, established that most were not into serious delinquency. But a minority were and the report concluded, 'Are our kids out of control? The answer is no, but there is a substantial minority of children who are neglected. You can deduce from that that those children are more likely to get involved in crime if there is nobody checking up on them.' (Painter, cited in *The Guardian*, 2 March 1993.) Neglected youngsters need not just to be checked up on but to be given the kind of unconditional, resourceful friendship displayed by the Major and his wife. Such friendship is within the capacities of many residents of the inner cities and estates where vulnerable youngsters are most likely to be found.

Befriending schemes

In an earlier chapter, Home-Start was described as a scheme in which ordinary but committed adults offered friendship to young parents in order to support them in the care of their children. In like manner, there are schemes through which friendship is given to young people.

Children North East, a charity based in Newcastle-upon-Tyne, has developed a visiting project called Homebase. With some financial backing from the local authority, it uses volunteers to befriend young people aged sixteen to twenty-one who have left public care. Homebase gives training to the volunteers on matters such as how to communicate with young people, how to react to difficult and uncooperative behaviour, how to deal with questions about income support and housing benefit. In order to avoid the impression that volunteers are imposed upon the care-leavers, the ball is put in the latter's court. They are allowed to refer themselves to the scheme and, if they do take on a volunteer, they determine the pace it goes at. Here are two examples of what has happened, quoted in Susan Mapp's article 'A Friend in Need', published in *Community Care*. Marjorie (not her real name), aged sixty, volunteered to visit a seventeen-year-old pregnant care-leaver:

I went to see her once or twice a week. It was a twenty-minute train journey. She had a lot of problems. She'd been abused as a child and the family had left her in the lurch.

When I was introduced to her, she was living with her boy friend, but they were not getting on. She wanted out. She was also on probation for stealing from shops. I met her on Sundays so I could make sure she got a meal. Friday nights they had no money left. She sold her radio to get some bread. She got a council flat and was pleased. I went with her to buy things for it. She had £600 leaving care grant from Newcastle and I advised her on spending it wisely. We found bargains and I passed on some baby clothes. She came to my house once. I could relate to her because I have had two daughters. My youngest is pregnant, but does not live nearby. And I had my first baby when I was seventeen. I think it is possible that her family have rallied round by now, but I wonder how long that will last. I haven't heard from her for quite a while, although I have written saying I am always here for her. She is the sort that will get in touch if she needs help. If not, she will just drop in. I don't take it to heart. You have to leave it up to them.

Dave, aged forty, visited a twenty-one-year-old male care-leaver. He recorded,

He lived in a council flat on an estate and went to college. He had acquaintances there, but no real friends. I am a full-time

house husband at the moment, so I was able to visit him twice a week. He was a very lonely lad and used to get depression, which he is on tablets for.

His father would go for him when he was drunk. He set up home by himself but was forever short of money and in arrears with his gas, electricity, and water. I persuaded them to let him pay the bills off in instalments.

He would ring me and say: 'Are you doing anything?' He'd never ask directly if I'd go round, as he was afraid of rejection.

At a tribunal we tried to get his income support and housing benefit increased, just by another couple of pounds, so he could get wallpaper and paint to improve the flat. He had about £12 a week to live on, and out of that he had to get his fares of £2 or £3 a day.

I represented him, and the social security people put their case. We didn't get the money. A woman on the panel said: 'If you need clothes or furniture, go to the Salvation Army.' He was in tears and I had to bite my tongue. He's back with his parents now—he couldn't survive on the money he was getting.

These two volunteers did not attempt to control the young people and knew that they could not bring about great changes in their living conditions. But they expressed genuine concern, attempted to understand the problems from the youngsters' point of view, and gave practical help on budgeting and benefits. Probably the volunteers helped them cope during the sticky period immediately after leaving public care and before re-establishing contact with their natural families.

Possilpark

The Possilpark Befriending Project in Glasgow was established by a voluntary body, the Save the Children Fund, in co-operation with Strathclyde Regional Council. It links volunteers with youngsters who are referred to the project either because there is a likelihood that the Children's Hearings will place them under the statutory supervision of the Social Work Department or because they are already under supervision and are at risk of being removed from their families altogether. The aim of the scheme is to prevent the youngsters being drawn into—or further into—delinquent behaviour which will lead to statutory action being taken against them.

Volunteers who wish to become befrienders are initially reached by public advertisements. Applicants are then interviewed, references taken up and enquiries made about any criminal background. Those selected then have to complete an evening training course which gives understanding of the effects of neglect, abuse and separation on young people and discusses what should happen within the relationship between the befriender and the befriended. Two examples follow, in the words of volunteers, quoted in B. Wright's *Possilpark Befriending Project Report*, published by Save the Children. A female befriender writes,

I had been thinking of doing some kind of work in the community for a number of years—but was unsure of how I could be of use. I saw a poster for the Project at the University and thought—'I could do that!'

I think this kind of project is ideal. Firstly, it offered a choice of voluntary work and secondly, the Project provided social and financial assistance. I find all the staff friendly and helpful and would not hesitate to contact them. I am matched with Mary. Mary is a twelve-year-old who has learning difficulties and has rarely had the chance to leave her home environment—so I am trying to find something different for her to do every week. The kind of activities which we currently enjoy are cinema, ice-skating, baking, pony riding, cooking and painting. I feel our friendship is going really well. Every week improves as I learn what she can and cannot do, her likes and dislikes. And of course, every time she goes out and repeats experiences—like getting on the bus/tube—she gains confidence and pride at having acquired a new skill. Simple things like these and watching Mary being able to do them with ease brings the greatest sense of achievement and happiness to both of us. Apart from being her friend, I think this is where I can be most useful to Mary, to help her learn practical things like shopping, travelling and taking care of herself. Mary, on the other hand, seems to be quite comfortable with me and is not at all shy of holding my hand/arm when we are out or giving me hugs. She eagerly awaits my arrival and when the day is over she never wants to go home and tries to find clever excuses to prolong the inevitable.

A male befriender recorded,

I first got involved in the Project through a friend who was already a befriender. I work shifts in my job so I found that I have the spare time to offer to a commitment. I attended an induction training course along with other new volunteers.

I befriended a young boy called Malcolm. We have been meeting regularly for the last few months going out together. We have gone cycling, to the cinema, ten-pin bowling, swimming and have made various other visits. Malcolm was very quiet at first but now we find it easy to get along and have no problems talking to each other.

At the moment things are going well for Malcolm but he was getting into trouble with the Police, running away from home and sleeping rough. His parents were at their wits' end to know what could be done to help. I didn't have the answers but it seems that my involvement has helped to stabilise Malcolm's life and has helped me to understand some of the difficulties facing young people today.

I'll always remember the time we went to the Alien Wars Exhibition. It was set up like a space ship and, unknown to us, all the attendants were actors playing different parts. It was a bit frightening and Malcolm thought the safest place was to be beside the guide as he had a gun. But when the alien attacked the guide, Malcolm took off like a shot.

When I eventually found him outside in the street he assured me it had been brilliant but there was no way he was going back inside.

In its first year of operation, the Possilpark Befriending Project approved forty-seven volunteers, thirty-two female and fifteen male who then befriended fifty-eight youngsters, twenty-one females and thirty-seven males. The early indications are that the scheme does have a positive effect on the young people and the local authority is keen for it to continue.

Friendship in the community

Tom O'Neill met friendship within a hostel. The befriending schemes are agencies which match volunteers (from various locations) with young people usually referred by the local authority. My own experience has been with youngsters who are not referred but who got to know members of our projects because we all lived in the same neighbourhood and they attended the youth clubs. I have been with two neighbourhood projects, one in England and one in Scotland, and. I will illustrate the friendship work with an example from each.

Wyn

Wyn was thirteen when he joined the youth club. Quick-witted and cheerful, he was soon in charge of its café. He started to call regularly at our home so I soon dropped in to introduce myself to his parents. His dad was unemployed yet spent much of his time out of the house. His mum appeared to be the one who kept control and she indicated her pleasure that Wyn had joined the club and said she was pleased for him to visit our home.

Soon it became clear that Wyn had a number of problems. He did not want to spend much time in his own home yet, on the streets, drifted from friend to friend. He disliked school, where he had been placed in what he called 'the duffers' class'. However, his main problem was stealing. Other kids warned me that he was light-fingered. Then he came to tell me that he had been nicked for house-breaking and asked me to go to court with him. I accompanied Wyn and his mum—dad could not be found—to the juvenile court where he was fined.

The stealing continued, particularly shop lifting. Having formed a friendship with Wyn, I felt able to tackle him about it. Initially he denied having a problem yet soon he broke down in tears saying, 'I just can't stop, I want to but I can't stop.' My response was that if he really wanted to stop then eventually he would, that my colleague Dave Wiles (who lodged in our house) and I were on his side, and that he could always turn to us for help. Wyn seized the chance of relating with adults and called continuously—he came five times on Christmas Day. I continued to see his mum although, when I called, his dad was rarely in. When I asked about Wyn and his dad, she shrugged her shoulders and said that the two just could not communicate. Soon after, when Wyn was prosecuted for shop lifting, I spoke to the magistrates on his behalf. They placed him on probation and recommended that the probation officer should encourage Wyn's close involvement with our project.

By the age of fourteen, Wyn was in trouble with his parents, teachers and the police. He seemed to be condemned by so many people in his life that Dave and I decided to give him more responsibilities within the club as a sign of our belief in him. He became a helper at one of the junior clubs and also accompanied us when we went to meetings to talk about the project. He did his tasks well—for which we were able to praise him—and identified strongly with us and the project. He went through periods of calm and stability although an explosion of emotions was always near the surface. He was taking an increasing amount of time off school, often giving flimsy excuses like it was too cold or wet—although the weather never prevented him hanging about the streets or coming to the clubs.

One afternoon, I refused to let him into our house,

saying that he should be at school. He argued that he did not have to attend as it was just games. However, when I said I would phone to confirm that he could stay away, he stormed off angrily.

Money went missing from my wallet. Sitting in the van, I told him that I had been watching him. He snarled,

'That's right. Blame me. If anything goes wrong, it's always me.'

'No. But today I counted my money carefully. You've been the only one in the house and £3 has gone.'

'I tell you I f— haven't got it.'

I persisted and reiterated that friendship had to be built on trust and truth. He gave in.

'OK, I took it. It's all right for you. I tell you, when I went to get some dinner at home there was nothing. My brothers had taken the lot.'

I retrieved the money and we talked about his poor relationships at home. The talk had little effect for, a few days later, his mum appeared angrily proclaiming that Wyn had nicked her purse and disappeared. After sleeping rough for one night, he returned. I went with him to his mum whose anger had been replaced by concern over his absence. I tried to explain to Wyn that his mum's anxiety was an indication of her love for him.

Before the year was out, he was in trouble again at school. His class teacher phoned to inform me that he and another boy had been stealing school dinner tickets and then selling them at a lower price than the school. The police were called and another prosecution followed. I feared he would be sent away, but the magistrates, aware of our attempts to help him, imposed a fine of £40.

Yet it was not all negative. He kept accurate accounts for the club's cafe and we entrusted him with the profits to purchase the latest Top of the Pops records. At the summer camps, he was extremely helpful, putting up tents and doing the cooking. In between, he continued to come to our home nearly every day to watch TV, to join in meals and to chat with my Scottish wife, whom he fondly called Mrs Haggis. He said that by spending time with us he was stopped from going thieving with other lads.

At times, Dave and I worried that Wyn was becoming too dependent upon us and that we were drawing him away from his own family. When, at last, I found both his parents in and discussed the matter they responded that I was not keeping him away from them as he was rarely in anyway, and that they would sooner know that he was safe in the clubs or at our home. Then, for a couple of months, Wyn obtained a washing-up evening job in a restaurant. The money in his pocket and the status of doing a job proved beneficial to him—and he paid off his fine.

By the age of fifteen, Wyn's major difficulties centred upon school, where his eruptions of temper were directed at staff, followed by frequent truanting. His helpful and concerned teacher approached us to suggest that Wyn did a work experience placement with the project. We were glad to co-operate and the three parties, the teacher, Wyn, and myself signed an agreement that he would work three days a week at the project on condition that he attended school regularly on the other two days. It worked well. Wyn revelled in his position as an assistant project worker, organized the football team, prepared the clubs, washed the minibus, got the soup ready at lunchtime, and supervised games at the junior clubs. One evening, when a younger boy was determined to do a break-in, Wyn persuaded him against it and took him for some chips.

Wyn kept his promise about attending school but sometimes the teachers must have wished he hadn't. Following a couple of outbursts, he was banned from a catering course which he enjoyed. He was so disruptive and out of control that a senior teacher brought him to our home. After he had calmed down, we went over the incident. I asked him to draw it in cartoon form, which introduced an element of humour. He explained that the teacher had made him look small and picked on him. I explained that his failure to control his temper (even if provoked) could have adverse effects on him, particularly as he was thinking of taking up catering as a career. Finally, he wrote a letter of apology to the teacher and was accepted back on the course.

In his last term at school, Wyn chose the project as his special subject in the examinations. He had to write about it, which he found difficult, and speak about it—which he found easier, for he was never lost for words.

Wyn's life seemed to be on a smoother path. He appreciated our friendship and brought in goodies which he had cooked, often presenting them to my wife with a hug. I pointed out that the food and the hugs were expressions of his affection and we discussed how he could display his affection for his mum and dad. We continued to consider his stealing and drew a chart which measured how long he went without stealing or losing his temper. But, as so often with Wyn, it was the calm before the storm. Our friendship was about to be shattered.

Dave and I had been to visit my son who was seriously ill in hospital with osteomyelitis. My wife was staying in the ward. On our return, Dave came down from his room looking shaken and holding an empty cash box. The youth club's holiday deposits had gone. Being in our house so often, Wyn would have known where it was kept. Moreover, one of the front door keys had gone missing. Heavy-hearted, I made my way up to his home. He was in but his mum immediately said it must have been Wyn. Eventually, Wyn was found and brought home. He swore, raged, denied it. His older brother wanted to beat the truth out of him. I stopped him. Sick with worry about my son, devastated that anyone should steal from us while we were at the hospital, I wanted to pack it all in.

A knock on the door. Wyn laid the money on the table except for a few quid which he had spent. Some parents wanted me to go to the police. Instead I banned him from our home for three months. The club members refused to let him go on the holiday. It was never quite the same again. Wyn left school.

All this was seventeen years ago. What has happened to Wyn? Stormy home relationships, low-income family, truancy, difficulties with authority, repeated offending— he possessed many of the predictors for a criminal career and prison.

I now live in Glasgow but have always kept in touch with him. Last year, while down south, I went to visit him. He met me at the station and drove me to a hotel for tea. He is the manager of a group of shops, a house owner, has had no trouble with the police since his teens. Why? Wyn thanks our project. I consider other factors were important. One key feature was that on leaving school he obtained a fulfilling job in a joiners. The manager took a kind but firm interest in him and spotted his capacity for selling and organizing. Promotion followed. With status and money, what was the point of nicking? More, he was able to afford the next crucial step—marriage. A job he valued, a decent salary, a steady relationship were vital factors in steering Wyn away from crime. Sadly, today, youngsters like him have much less chance of obtaining a job and being able to afford a home and marriage.

What part did our friendship play? It helped to keep Wyn in the community over the thirteen- to sixteen-year-old phase. Dave and I were always near and available when he was explosive. Our many conversations contributed to his efforts to control his behaviour. His daily participation in the project's activities provided an alternative to illegal behaviour. The responsibilities he was given in the clubs improved his self-image. Interestingly, he also says that during the work experience we made him work hard within a routine and so prepared him for employment. His offending was slowed. And when he did appear in court, I was able to speak about him from daily knowledge and offer continuing help within his neighbourhood.

If Wyn had gone into custody, he would have entered

a delinquent environment and would not have been around to take that job. His own assessment is that he would have been on the track for prison.

Arnold

My friendship with Wyn occurred some years ago and hence it has been possible to follow him into adulthood. The relationship with Arnold has been in more recent years when I have been working with a neighbourhood project in Glasgow.

Arnold did not experience an easy life even before he moved to our estate. He never knew his father and lived with his mum, Vera, step-dad, Jim, and two younger brothers. Vera was a caring mother who struggled with determination to look after her children but she faced enormous difficulties. Her partner, Jim, was amenable when sober but bad-tempered when drinking. They had depended upon income support for years and, when Jim was drinking heavily, Vera was at her wits' end to feed the family. Yet she remained loyal to her partner. She had already suffered one broken relationship from Arnold's dad and she did not want her two younger boys to be apart from their natural father, Jim.

Arnold appeared adversely affected by the loss of his own father in two ways. First, he resented the fact that he did not know him. When he sought information about his dad from Vera she found it difficult to talk. Second, it led to Arnold having an uneasy relationship with Jim. To be sure, Jim did make some efforts but his hasty temper made Arnold wary of him, while he complained that he was not treated the same as his step-brothers.

A volunteer helper at our youth clubs was a neighbour of the family and soon brought Arnold along. He became a regular member yet did not participate much in the games. His own outbursts and sharp tongue made him unpopular with some boys and Arnold would complain that he was picked on. Although he was eleven years old, he was thin and not good at defending himself. Instead, he would retreat to a corner and sulk. He got on best with the adults, especially our project leader, Graham Hammond and myself. Usually he would linger after the clubs closed, help tidy up, and then walk me home in the expectation that I'd ask him up for a glass of orange and a biscuit.

When Arnold heard that one of the clubs was going camping for a week in the summer, he was keen to go. I said I'd have to discuss it with his parents and called to see them. Step-dad Jim answered my questions with a grunt. Vera was delighted that he was attending the clubs, saying that he had never stuck at anything before. She was keen for him to go to the camp and, when I mentioned the costs, replied that she would ask her social worker to pay. She explained that the Social Work Department was worried about Arnold's behaviour at school and home and suggested I had a word with the social worker (whom I already knew). I did so and the department was pleased to finance Arnold.

The camp was not an unqualified success. Arnold, now twelve and older than some of the other campers, seemed more immature. He constantly moaned about the other boys in his tent while they criticized his lack of ability at sport and his lack of enthusiasm. Before long, Arnold was refusing to participate and, when efforts were made to persuade him, he sulked and on two occasions ran away. The second time he was missing for several hours, and we spent a lot of time looking for him. Yet he related well to some of the camp staff and particularly liked hanging around and helping in the cookhouse. By the end of the week, he was making greater efforts to join in with the other youngsters. On his return home, he declared that the holiday was 'brill' and that he wanted to go again.

The flat in which the family was living was damp and in need of many repairs. Eventually the housing department boarded it up and moved the family some three miles away, although still on the same estate. With the aid of the Salvation Army van, I helped Vera and Jim move. They were pleased with the new flat, although it meant that the boys had to change school again. Arnold was upset at not being so near to the clubs and expressed his feelings in cheekiness towards his mum and in uncooperative behaviour. After talking with the family, we agreed that twice a week he should get the bus straight from school and come to my place for tea before attending club; afterwards Graham or I would give him a lift home. The arrangement worked smoothly. Obviously, Arnold was coming not so much for the clubs but for the company, for the friendship. I began also to take him swimming with two or three other boys. Initially he was terrified of the water, then, growing in confidence, he took a few strokes. He glowed at our praise and soon he was jumping in, diving, and swimming strongly. Swimming became one of the enjoyments of his life. Yet once again his young life was to be disrupted.

One evening, Arnold phoned me, 'Bob, mum says can you come and see us. We're in bed and breakfast.' And so they were. Their family of five had been moved to a basement room in a hostel some seven miles away. Descending the stairs to their room, I saw a notice on the wall which read 'No children upstairs. No playing on the stairs.' As I entered, I caught sight of Arnold sitting on a bed, his head cupped in his hands, staring sightlessly at a flickering black and white TV. Vera and Jim, and later their social worker, told me what had happened. One of Arnold's step-brothers had been allegedly sexually assaulted by a neighbour who then, with his mates, threatened Vera with violence if the police were called in. The police did come but eventually it was decided that there was not enough evidence to prosecute. In order to protect Vera and Jim, the authorities had moved the whole family out.

I talked with Vera and Jim about what they wanted. Clearly they did not want to stay in bed and breakfast. If re-housed by the council, they knew that they would be offered a place on one of Glasgow's four large estates. They reasoned that they did not know anybody elsewhere so they might as well go back to their home estate where, at least, Arnold could attend the clubs. They argued that it would be best not to go back to the same street but to be very near to the clubs and the project. The social worker agreed that this was a sensible ploy and we approached the housing department.

To our dismay, Vera and Jim were informed that, as they had been unsatisfactory tenants in the past, they would have to wait several months before they could be moved. At Vera and Jim's request, I took up their case with housing officials, councillors and the MP. To no avail. The whole family was suffering from being cooped up in a small space. Vera and Jim were arguing. The child who had been allegedly abused was showing such signs of disturbance that the social worker looked for some therapeutic treatment. Arnold was most upset. He disliked his new school and often truanted. Jim was increasingly irritated with him.

To relieve the tension, I began collecting Arnold three times a week for the clubs and swimming and returning him afterwards—a task which involved a fourteen-mile round trip each time. When at the bed and breakfast, he constantly phoned me and was clearly very unhappy. Finally, as the family reached desperation point, I wrote to the paper about the matter. This course is a last option, for it invariably angers officials. Sure enough, the director of housing immediately replied with a letter trying to justify his officials' actions. Yet the next day, Vera and Jim were told that they would be re-housed shortly. Within a few days they were in a flat in our district.

There followed the most fruitful and enjoyable time of our friendship with Arnold. Living so close, he could pop in frequently to see me and Graham. He didn't need an excuse to call, he just came for a game of cards, an apple, a chat. Vera also became a regular visitor. Her washing machine broke down and, being unable to afford a repair, she brought her washing over every other day. I introduced her to the day care centre where a place was found for her youngest child. Meanwhile, the local headmistress had extended a warm welcome to Arnold and his step-brother. His class teacher gave him much time and soon established an excellent rapport with him. Despite these positive efforts towards him, Arnold was still inclined to flare up and, at times, ran away from the school. The headmistress invited Vera in to discuss Arnold's behaviour and, at her request, I accompanied her. It was agreed that, when Arnold ran away, the head would phone me. She did so and often I was able to find him, calm him down, and return him.

As with Wyn years before, I did not want to come between Arnold and his family. I talked the matter over with them and suggested that we all went out together. Vera was pleased and, at times, she, the three children and I went swimming, to the park, or to the cinema together. But not Jim. He said he was glad for the others to go out but that he had other things to do. The 'other things' could include drinking with his friends. Meanwhile, my friendship with and conversations with Arnold deepened. He was able to express his grief and anger about not knowing his natural father. We also went over his difficulty in controlling his temper and his troubles with other children. I pointed out that he seemed to regard other children as rivals but that adults could like him at the same time as they liked others. We tried to devise means of controlling his outbursts like, when provoked, walking away and saying nothing for five minutes.

During our talks, I assured Arnold of my concern for him and told him that he could turn to me at any time. In the following months, he often did but once I let him down. One afternoon I was watching a Rangers v. Celtic cup tie on TV when he buzzed the door. I told him to go away and come back. Later Vera appeared looking for him. She explained that she and Jim had told him off several times and ordered him to stay in. In a huff,

Arnold jumped out of the window and had been missing for several hours. Feeling guilty that I had turned him away, I searched but with no success. As it got dark and late, Vera informed the police. After 10 p.m., Arnold came to my door. After a short talk, I walked him up to his home. The police soon arrived and loudly warned him that he was going to end up in prison unless he changed his ways. All this could have been avoided if I had kept my promise that he could turn to me at any time.

Soon after, Vera and Jim were summoned to a Children's Hearing. Social workers, worried about the alleged abuse and Arnold's behaviour, wanted the opinion of the panel about the family. Vera was terrified that the children would be removed from her and asked me to attend. Jim should also have attended but, at the last minute, declared that he was too ill to go.

At the hearing, the social worker explained her anxieties about the children. Vera, very nervous, managed to express her concern for them. I went over the involvement of our project, pointed out my own nearness to the family, and mentioned some of the strong points about it. The panel members were worried that one of the boys had been in a position to be abused by a neighbour and considered that Arnold's behaviour was a symptom of future delinquency.

The boys were placed on home supervision which meant that they were not to be removed from home but that the social worker would now be obliged to visit and report on the family whereas previously she had done so in a voluntary capacity. Simultaneously, they expressed appreciation of the project and requested that our services should continue to be offered to the family.

In the summer, the fourteen-year-old Arnold went with the club to its annual camp once more, with the Social Work Department paying the fee. He was much better behaved, perhaps because he had got to know some of the camp leaders and had been looking forward to seeing them again. He was by no means an enthusiastic participant in the team games but he enjoyed himself. He often rode around the field on a bike in the company of another boy and volunteered to do camp tasks with the adults. We were able to praise him for his improvement, and Vera, too, was pleased to receive news of his improvements.

Vera needed some good news, for her relationship with Jim was not going well. His increasing drinking made even greater demands on their limited income. Some weekends she found herself penniless and, reluctantly, had to ask me for some beans and spuds until the giro arrived on Monday. Unknown to Vera, Jim was also financing his booze by borrowing from loan sharks. When he could not repay, the heavies burst into their flat and gave Jim a beating. The terrified Arnold leapt through the window and fled. Vera rushed round to our flat where we phoned the police.

After Jim was treated at hospital, the police interviewed him. He said nothing, for he was too scared of further reprisals. The heavies then threatened to burn the flat unless Jim repaid his escalating debt. The police, ascertaining what was happening, advised the housing department to move the family out. The department acted swiftly and soon they were in another flat in an estate several miles away. Vera loyally stuck with her man.

Arnold was badly shaken by the violence and the move. Once again he had to start a new school. Once again I started the process of picking him up twice a week for tea and the clubs. Within a few months, the family were on the move again. Jim's enemies tracked him down and forced their way into the flat. Fortunately for Jim, he was out at the time but Vera and the children once more experienced the threats and verbal aggression. This time they were transported completely away from Glasgow and to another town. It became impossible to see Arnold regularly. Now fifteen, Arnold continued to phone me regularly and has been able to come on the camp once a year. Occasionally, I am able to visit the family when in their area and was delighted to learn that Jim had stopped his drinking.

My friendship with Arnold lasted four years. I had wanted to be involved with the whole family, and did achieve a trusting relationship with Vera. But I failed to engage Jim. We talked, drank tea together, sometimes I gave him a lift to various places, yet I always felt he wanted to keep me at a distance. This was his choice, for I took pains to explain to the family that I possessed no statutory powers and that my involvement with them depended entirely upon them. So, within this limitation, what did the friendship achieve for Arnold?

First, I believe it gave him some stability. He lived in a world of constant change, of changing homes, neighbour-hoods, schools and friends. I hope that for four years I was someone who did not change, who was always there, a small piece of security in an insecure life.

Second, it probably gave him a refuge. Often Arnold wanted to escape: to escape from over-crowded rooms, from family arguments, from the threat of violence, from the sneers of other children. At times he just ran away, walked for miles, once jumped on a train. Our friendship provided an alternative, a safe place and a safe person to turn to at moments of stress.

Third, it offered a non-threatening sounding board. Arnold understood that I could not force him to go to school and had no powers to remove him from his home. Perhaps the combination of my concern and my lack of threat encouraged him to unload some of his deeper fears and anxieties. I responded with, I hope, understanding and advice. I tried to get him to consider the effects of his actions on himself and others. I tried to clarify some of his confusion about his own background. I wanted him to perceive something of his own abilities and likeability.

Fourth, our friendship constituted an avenue to some of the everyday things of life which should be available to all children. It led to the youth clubs, swimming, the cinema, holidays. These activities are a part of growing up, yet he had been in danger of missing them.

Our friendship endeavoured to give Arnold some stability, a safe place, a sounding board, and social stimulation. It has not been the crucial influence on his life for that springs from his relationships with his family. But it may have been of value during a critical phase of his life and so may have helped to prevent him going down those paths which lead to distress, maladjustment and delinquency.

There is a postscript to the above paragraphs. During the year in which this book has been written, I have often spoken to Arnold on the phone. I arranged for him to go with some of our local youngsters on a holiday. He enjoyed it, partly because he met old friends again, partly because it contained horseriding, which he loves. He had grown considerably since I last saw him and I realized he was almost a young man. He likes living in the country. The future is brighter.

I may have given the impression that friendships always have a successful outcome. Not so. I spent hours with one unstable teenager, went to court with him, involved him in our project. He seemed to respond and convinced me that his delinquency was a thing of the past. But either he relapsed or he had been conning me all along for, after a while, he began stealing to feed his drug habit. Late one night, he wandered into our home and asked for money. I refused, knowing it would go on drugs. He then threatened me with a knife before storming out with his final shot, 'You must be the worst friend in the world.' Later he finished up homeless and on the streets. Others went to prison. Being a resourceful friend may end in pain, heartache, rejection and a sense of failure. Yet it also gives the potential to be a change-maker, to be a means of engaging with vulnerable young people to enable them to draw back from delinquency.

Rules for the resourceful

I have had a number of friendships with young people. Not many have been with the intensity of those with Wyn and Arnold. However, they all have the same essence, namely the promotion of a relationship between an older person with a younger one, in order to help the latter. Of course, as a full-time and later a part-time project worker, I have been in a position to give many hours to young people. Yet the medium of friendship is not restricted to full-timers. Nor is it just for the professionals, for the befriending schemes demonstrate that a great variety of people can be involved.

Possibly readers of this chapter can envisage themselves as befrienders. In their neighbourhoods they can see youngsters who need guidance and support, and believe they possess the resources of emotional stability, personal integrity and skills in communication which could be of use. I hope so. But resourceful friendship should not be entered into lightly, because if the befriender does not sustain the friendship then the result can be a sense of rejection for the befriended. If undertaken, however, these basic rules of befriending are worth following.

Befriending should be from within an agency

Befrienders should not be lone rangers who just select kids to take out. Adults who take an interest in other people's children will be objects of suspicion unless they are approved by, accountable to, and supervised by a responsible agency, be it a youth club, church, Sunday school, community association or specific befriending scheme. The agency should supply support and guidance to the befriender and may well be a resource to which the befriended can sometimes be brought to enjoy communal activities.

Friendships with youngsters should be formed only with parental permission

One boy often came to our clubs and began popping in to see me. I have a rule that no child can come into our flat unless I know the parents. I had chatted with his mother in the street and then called to speak with her. She told me that her husband was in prison and that she welcomed her son seeing me. Later she initiated a discussion about the boy's stealing at home and poor behaviour at school. We went to the school where the headmistress considered that some of his problems were associated with his backwardness in reading. We all agreed that once a week I should go into the school to give him individual tuition in reading and once a month take mother and son to visit the father in prison.

Even with permission, the befriender must remain sensitive to the parents. An unemployed man who encouraged his son's involvement nevertheless subsequently admitted to me that he sometimes felt very jealous that I could give his son activities which were beyond his pocket. If I had possessed more sensitivity, I should have taken the father along on some of the outings.

Befriending should have a clear purpose

Taking youngsters out, having them in for coffee, chatting together, are useful because all youngsters should have enjoyable leisure periods and because they help to build up a friendship. But these are stepping stones which are intended to deal with a specific need or difficulty such as combating truancy, aggression, isolation, withdrawal, stealing, violence. Moreover, the purpose should not be hidden from the young person. Sometimes, especially with a younger child, the befriender is filling a gap in a home. For instance, within a one-parent family, the befriender may take on roles, such as mending the bike, taking the youngster to the park, visiting the cinema, which the lone parent just does not have the time to do. Of course, the young person will probably benefit and the lone parent be glad of a break, but the danger is that the child may see the befriender as a permanent replacement for the parent who is not there. The truth, the purpose, the length of time the friendship is to last , must be honestly discussed with children and parents at the start, or misunderstanding and pain could result when the friendship ends.

Friendships are often best made in co-operation with another befriender

Thus Dave Wiles and I were together not just in the running of youth clubs but also in the exercise of resourceful friendship. Usually one was the leading befriender who made the closest relationship with the young person in question. But the second befriender would often be around and would usually come (with another youngster) to the swimming, the game of cards, the outing. Sometimes a youngster wanted to discuss his problems just with me, but I still preferred it if Dave was in another part of the house. The involvement of a second befriender has the additional advantage that he or she can provide support, advice and insights concerning progress. I have been fortunate in always having a colleague with whom to share befriending. I realize that others will not always have that advantage but, if possible, befrienders, like the early disciples of Jesus, will find that they work best in pairs.

Befriending should only be undertaken with the backing of spouses, partners and, if relevant, of children

Youngsters who are befriended may well take up a family's time, call just when a meal is starting, spill coffee over the best carpet, annoy the people next door. If potential befrienders live with their families then they must consider the likely effects on all family members before starting.

Resourceful friendship is one of the most demanding, effective and rewarding means of helping potential and actual delinquents. It is demanding, in that befrienders invest their own time and emotions and there are times when they feel that their time is wasted and their emotions trampled upon. It is effective, in that resourceful friends tend to engage with youngsters in their teenage years when the pressures to commit crimes are at their greatest. It is rewarding, as other befrienders, as well as myself, will testify: to have used friendship as a means of preventing a young person getting into trouble or of steering a delinquent out of the practice of crime is a source of tremendous personal satisfaction.

E L E V E N

Proclamation

What has this book said so far? In this final chapter, a summary is in order.

Delinquency is rooted in the family. Children are more prone to committing crimes if their parents have been unable or unwilling to meet their physical, material and emotional needs; if they have not given them warm relationships, social stimulation, consistent yet kindly discipline, and appropriate values. In addition, disruptions to family life through separations and divorce and the pressures associated with single parenthood can make it harder—although not impossible—for parents to apply the best child-rearing methods. Sometimes, too, the disruption caused by removal from home into public care can prove damaging to children, despite the skilled efforts of caring staff.

But the family does not exist in a vacuum. There are forces outside it which directly influence children's functioning and which can help or hinder parents in their child-rearing tasks. Attention was drawn to:

◆ **PEER PRESSURES**
The influence of friends can be for good or ill, helping young people to resist or, by contrast, drawing them into delinquency.

◆ **THE MEDIA, PARTICULARLY TV AND VIDEOS**

Although many programmes are both enjoyable and positive, there is concern over the frequency in which they display lifestyles which condone family break-ups, which glorify crime, and in which violence and sexual lust are presented in such graphic ways as to encourage repetition by youngsters who are already pre-disposed in these directions. They lead into temptation.

◆ **PUBLIC MORALITY**

The lack of fidelity, integrity and honesty amongst some public figures is now transmitted into every home. Moreover, leading people often seem motivated more by greed and self-interest than by a desire to serve others. The outcome is the creation of a moral climate in which dishonesty and individual self-interest become prominent and which, amongst some young people, must be like a green light to delinquency.

◆ **SOCIAL DEPRIVATIONS**

Most poor people are not criminals yet an association does exist between poverty and criminality. Long-term poverty can undermine the efforts of parents to bring up their children in satisfactory ways, while unemployment with its sense of futility, its experience of boredom and its lack of money for necessities, can drive some young people into delinquency.

These experiences and pressures which, in combination, can push some youngsters towards delinquency can be illustrated, in a crude way, in Diagram 1 over the page.

In response to the pressures which provoke delinquency, this book has argued that action can be taken to modify them. Amongst the suggested means of intervention are the provision of stimulating experiences for infant children, support and friendship for

DIAGRAM 1: PRESSURES TOWARDS DELINQUENCY

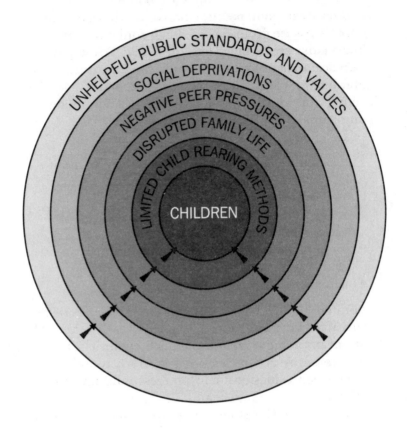

parents under stress, constructive leisure outlets for youngsters, and resourceful friendships for teenagers on the verge of, or already into, delinquency. However, these interventions do not touch upon two of the most serious pressures, namely the influence of public values and of social deprivations. Lack of morality at the top and intensive poverty at the bottom makes for a society in which crime does more easily take hold. What can ordinary citizens do? I suggest they can make proclamation—that is, they can act by word and deed—in three spheres: the national, the local and the personal.

National action

All citizens can join political parties and participate in national pressure groups which lobby for better standards in the media and which, like the Child Poverty Action Group, campaign for a reduction in poverty and the establishment of a fairer society. The immediate justification for attacking poverty and its accompanying unemployment and social deprivations is that it would alleviate many of the pressures and conditions which push some young people towards crime. However, the case for reducing both poverty and crime should, I believe, also rest on broader grounds of principle.

As I mentioned in Chapter 1, I believe that all people are a part of the family of God and all are of equal importance to him. It follows that all people are kin: we all have the same Creator and hence are related to each other. The deduction is that our relationships with each other should be that of mutuality which, as I have elaborated in my book *A New Deal for Social Welfare*, means that we want the very best for each other. The 'best' means being a member of a society in which crime and poverty are at a minimum and which is built on the God-revealed values of fidelity, honesty and love for our neighbour.

I write from Christian convictions but I believe the above objectives will be acceptable to many people of other faiths and, indeed, of none. If so, their campaigning or proclamation within political parties and pressure groups has to be in two directions. One is to establish the principles or values which make both poverty and delinquency unacceptable. The other is to propose practical policies which can reduce both.

The range of policies which can attack poverty cannot be detailed here. But mention can be made of the views of the collection of experts who made up the Commission on Social Justice (1994). Its proposals to establish a more just society included:

ACTION

- the alleviation of poverty by legislation to set a Minimum Income Standard;

- an increase in employment by vocational training more geared to job vacancies, along with wage subsidies to persuade employers to take on the long-term unemployed;

- the reduction of poverty for those in work by the establishment of a minimum wage;

- the expansion of better housing by local Housing Companies to develop social housing for rent and by a National Housing Bank to finance new accommodation;

- fiscal policies to 'redistribute resources from richer to poorer members of society'.

It may well be objected that the country could not afford such proposals. Not so. The foremost British expert on poverty, Professor Peter Townsend, explains that if the wealthiest 20 per cent lost a fifth of their disposable income, then the incomes of the poorest 20 per cent could be doubled. Poverty could be dramatically reduced if our society held and acted upon principles which desired a greater sharing of its resources.

It may well also be objected that a redistribution of resources might harm the economy. The economist Will Hutton disagrees. He argues that greater purchasing power in the hands of people who will spend it, not on luxuries but on food, clothing, furniture, child care will help to revive the economy and boost employment. As Hutton concludes, 'The fight against poverty is not only a moral injunction—the just society begets the sound economy.' Of course, it is not claimed that anti-poverty measures will rid society of the scourge of delinquency. Poverty is just one of many factors which contribute to the social conditions in which crime will flourish. Moreover, some human selfishness and greed will always persist, whatever the social environment. But there is some overlap between delinquency and poverty and the abolition of extreme social deprivations would enable more parents to improve their child-rearing methods, more children to have a stable and stimulating up-bringing, more teenagers to have jobs, and fewer young people reduced to the desperation which pushes them into anti-social behaviour.

Local action

Political action for reform, at central and local government level, may seem too long-term for some citizens. More immediately, they could identify with local community groups which have an immediate effect on the alleviation of poverty amongst low-income people, as the following examples show.

Credit unions

These can be associations of residents of socially-deprived areas who save together and then lend out to members at low interest rates. In the district where I live, the credit union has over 600 members who pay no more than 1 per cent interest per month for their loans. The credit union has enabled them to improve their family life by purchasing cookers, furniture, holidays, Christmas presents, and so on, at low interest rates, instead of the high ones charged by legal money money-lenders and the excessive rates charged by loan sharks.

Food co-ops

These involve local people acting together to bulk-buy food from markets and cash and carry stores and then to re-sell it to members at low prices. Families can save £4–£5 a week on their budgets and so improve the quality and quantity of their food intake.

Day care centres

These provide environments where small children learn to interact with each other under the purposeful leadership of trained staff. Knowing their children are safe, parents are then freed to seek jobs. Lone parents in particular need day care in order to improve their incomes via employment.

Community groups are vital because of their immediate practical effects. They also have another significance, in that their members often display an altruism, a fellowship, a readiness to make sacrifices for others, which is a challenge to the selfishness, individualism and materialism of much of contemporary Britain. They proclaim the mutuality which could make for a more responsible, more equal, less criminal society.

Around two-and-a-half million people give time to community groups in Britain. Unfortunately, they are often financially weak. Their supporters tend to be poor; they lack the fund-raising machinery, the PR departments, the royal patrons of the national voluntary societies which receive over 90 per cent of all voluntary donations. Further, the decline of local government means that its grants to local groups have withered.

It may be that readers of this book do not reside in areas where they can participate in the community groups which are of such direct, practical relevance to families with low incomes. But they may well belong to churches, clubs and associations which could provide regular financial backing for the groups. I can think of one community group in our area which was constantly subjected to break-ins. Then an affluent suburban church paid for the group to install an alarm which was connected with the police station. Their problem was virtually solved.

Interestingly, the Commission on Social Justice recognized both the value and the needs of local groups. It proposes that the government establish a National

Community Regeneration Agency which would oversee Community Development Trusts in 250 deprived locations. The Commission is somewhat vague in its discussion of the functions and composition of the trusts, but hopefully they would contain representatives from the inner cities and peripheral council estates , who would distribute funds to groups which are truly in the hands of, and of direct use to, residents. If each trust allocated, say, £3 million a year, the effect could be dramatic, leading to an expansion not just of those groups tackling poverty but also the kinds of projects mentioned in earlier chapters which supply befriending schemes and youth clubs. The expansion would also allow some to take on staff and so reduce unemployment in the very districts where jobs are most scarce.

Personal action

Lastly, consideration must be given to the ways in which we conduct our own lives. The pages of newspapers are full of details about the failings of individuals: of those who live in luxury while ignoring the plight of those who endure abject poverty; of those who publicly uphold family values yet in private have fathered children out of wedlock; of those who decry crime yet use their positions to unscrupulously fill their own pockets. Their personal examples contribute to a moral climate in which greed, dishonesty and selfishness is encouraged. Yet individual action can also be a means of proclaiming a better vision for society.

An outstanding example of one whose life lived up to his principles is George Lansbury. Born in 1859, Lansbury was brought up, often in poverty, in the East End of London. His unexpected conversion to Christianity came under the ministry of the Rev. Fenwick Kitto, the vicar of Whitechapel. Kitto's influence over Lansbury was exercised not through preaching, but through friendship, for Kitto, unlike many Anglican ministers of his time, gave priority to his poor parishioners. Lansbury later explained, in beautiful testimony, that 'nobody has ever had quite the same influence, in a way it is not possible to explain, on my wife and myself as he did. He entered into our lives, teaching us mainly by example.' Lansbury not only became a Christian but also appeared to model his style on that of Kitto—a person who expressed his faith in everyday practice.

Lansbury was also moved by the intense poverty of his time. He noted its effects on the ill-health, shattered home life, and, interestingly, the delinquency of his neighbourhood. He merged his Christianity and politics into what is now called Christian Socialism and was elected a councillor, then an MP, cabinet minister and finally leader of the Labour party. He died in 1940.

This is not the place to record Lansbury's political successes and failures, but rather the style of his life. Lansbury lived all his adult life in the East End and most of it in the same house in Bow Road. Whether out of parliament or as a cabinet minister, he refused to follow those who moved out to the more healthy and comfortable suburbs. This is not to say he lived in poverty, although he, his wife Bessie, and their large family lived modestly. Rather, he chose to stay close to those in greatest need. He would look out of his window and see poverty-stricken women walking with their ill-clad children and unemployed youngsters with little to do and he wanted to be alongside them. He once said to his friend Father John Groser, who in *Politics and Persons* recalled Lansbury's words:

John, I would sooner be here in Bow Road where the unemployed can put a brick through my window when they disagree with my activities, than be in some other place far away where they can only write a letter.

And occasionally the bricks did come, for his closeness did not mean easiness. But being near, he could not forget, could not slacken in his efforts to combat poverty. Being near, Lansbury was also able to work with his neighbours.

He co-operated with them in voluntary action, in campaigns, in rejoicings and in sorrows. They met together in their homes, in churches, on the streets. In his books, he lists the many ordinary people—dockers, brushmakers, postal workers, housewives—who were his friends, colleagues and fellow-participants. He wrote,

... my most cherished memories will be of the long, long years of work and pleasure, agitation and propaganda, carried on in company with these countless numbers of people, most of whom possess no money, but who do possess the greatest of God's gifts, the spirit of comradeship and loyalty to each other.

This involvement *with*, not just for, people, had a two-fold significance. First, it stimulated some low-incomed, often unemployed friends to develop their capacities as volunteers and office holders. Second, it gave prominence to what he called comradeship, others call fellowship, and I call mutuality.

Next, Lansbury was prepared to share his resources with those in need. His door could always be knocked upon. He constantly gave advice to distressed citizens as they came to see him about rent, the dole, and pensions. And, if necessary, he gave directly to those in desperate need. Indeed, in the early days of their marriage, his wife was sometimes dismayed when he gave to others while they were struggling with little money for their own children.

Not least, Lansbury refused to use his position to line his own pockets. When he was elected a Guardian to administer the Poor Law, he refused to participate in the seven-course meals served by inmates to officials. Indeed, he succeeded in abolishing them. As a politician, he would take no bribes and would push no interests for personal gain. He did not even want the higher pension to which he was entitled as a former cabinet minister. Yet Lansbury was rich in the influence he had upon others. He inspired others to live lives of integrity dedicated to the needs of the most needy. As I recorded in my life of George Lansbury, *Good Old George*, the later Speaker of the House of Commons, George Thomas, said of him, 'He was loved, he was really loved.'

We are not Lansburys. But his lifestyle does have implications for ordinary citizens who wish to modify poverty and uphold certain public values. Some, certainly not all, could endeavour to live close to low-income recipients, to participate in their projects and campaign with them for a fairer society. Whether alongside them or not, such citizens could refuse for themselves the kind of incomes and high standards of living which reinforce gross inequalities. They could regard resources as a gift to be shared, not as possessions to be accumulated. They could uphold standards of honesty and integrity at home and work. If thousands of citizens thus proclaimed their opposition to poverty, to greed, to dishonesty, to hypocrisy, they might well act as a counter to those prevailing forces which, by tolerating poverty and glorifying materialism, create the social conditions and moral attitudes which imperil family life, corrupt values and breed delinquency.

These proposals for reducing poverty and challenging public voices complete the suggestions for means of preventing delinquency. Taken with my other suggestions, they can be presented in Diagram 2 on the following page.

If implemented, these means of intervention would not abolish delinquency. But they could enable more parents to develop helpful child-rearing methods, give more children a better start in life, support more stressed parents through times of crises, provide healthy leisure for more youngsters, divert more teenagers away from trouble. In general, they could contribute to promoting conditions and values which encourage fulfilling and honest lives. Moreover, they are approaches which can be pursued by non-professionals, by residents of the inner cities, the council estates and the suburbs, within their membership of voluntary bodies, churches and community groups.

DIAGRAM 2: MEANS OF PREVENTING DELINQUENCY

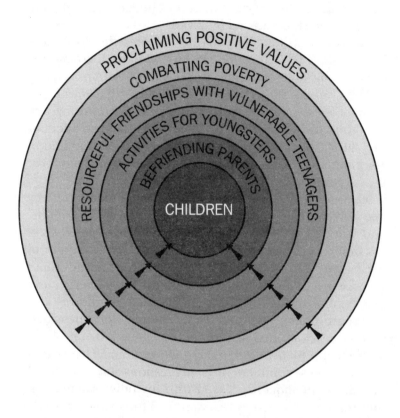

A few weeks ago, Wally Cripps phoned me, 'Bob, we've been burnt out, can you move us?' The Cripps' top-floor flat had gone up in flames, probably due to faulty wiring. They had escaped with their lives but little else. Neighbours gave them shelter and the housing department soon found them another flat. However, it could not provide transport, so the Cripps turned to me.

Mrs Cripps, terrified by the ordeal, would not not go back into the flat. I went with seventeen-year-old Wally and fifteen-year-old Sonia and, amidst burnt-out rafters, blackened walls and weakened floorboards, we put what we could into plastic bags and transported them to the new address. Before leaving, Wally looked around and said, 'Well, I'm not sorry to leave this place.' I knew what he meant. It was a street with high levels of crime and drug-taking. It contained a number of stable families and good parents, but they had to contend with many difficulties. The Cripps had had their door kicked in and their flat burgled on more than one occasion.

Mrs Cripps had borne three children, Millie, Wally and Sonia, before her husband disappeared. His heavy drinking and occasional violence had not made for an easy home life but at least he had been in work. Thereafter she was left to bring up the children on her own on state welfare benefits.

The eldest daughter, Millie, seemed most affected by her childhood instability and their life of near poverty. She never settled at school and frequently truanted as she got older. On leaving school, she spent much time out of the home with a distraught Mrs Cripps spending hours searching for her. She started to steal. Then she became pregnant and Mrs Cripps took on much of the responsibility of looking after newborn Alistair. Before long, it became evident that Millie was into heavy drugs. Days became nightmares. Millie did anything for her supplies, she stole from mum, went begging, shoplifting. She ended up in prison with Mrs Cripps lovingly bringing up Alistair.

Wally was different. He joined our clubs where he often got laughs by doing daft things. His behaviour, though never malicious, was erratic and, at the secondary stage, he was sent to a special dayschool. As he grew into his teens, he became more helpful and took on positions of responsibility both in the clubs and in a church which he joined. He is completely honest and, when he left school, I was pleased to write him a reference when he obtained a job in a fast food shop. Sonia too keeps out of trouble. She is more introverted than Wally and, when not at school, spends much time at home helping to look after the baby.

This family illustrates some of the themes of this book. The Cripps children appeared to become vulnerable to delinquency because the desertion of their father created family instabilities which cast them into poverty and made child-rearing difficult. Statutory services in the form of central government benefits and local government housing were essential in allowing the family to survive, although it was often a breadline existence, with Mrs Cripps never going on holiday and, for instance, being unable to afford a repair when the washing machine broke down. Perhaps it is not surprising that Millie did succumb, that she took on practices and values which led her into defiance, bad company, crime, drugs and, finally, prison. Yet, in the same family, in the same neighbourhood, Wally and Sonia have not become delinquent. Why?

Credit must be given to Mrs Cripps, who has been determined to keep her family together. At times she has nearly cracked up, has threatened to walk out, but somehow she has endured and given the children love and permanency. She was much helped by getting Wally and Sonia (and now Alistair) into a voluntary day care centre where they gained from the skills of the staff and the company of other children. Mrs Cripps was pleased when, later, Wally—and to a lesser extent, Sonia—joined our clubs, where they enjoyed leisure in a safe environment and went on the club holidays. At times, Mrs Cripps turned to the staff at the project for which I work when she felt at the end of her tether, emotionally or financially. In addition, Mrs Cripps had some good friends, like the neighbours who took them in when their flat was destroyed.

Perhaps Millie was unfortunate in bearing the brunt of the family's early misfortunes. Subsequently, it has survived through difficult times, thanks to a combination of Mrs Cripps' own strengths, the material provision from the welfare services, and the support of local projects and neighbours. As this book has stressed, the latter can play a part in helping vulnerable families to cope and to prevent their children being drawn into delinquency.

Lastly, the contribution of Wally and Sonia themselves should not be overlooked. They are individuals who have chosen to take advantage of the local youth clubs, to help with Alistair, and, in Wally's case, to persist in finding a job after numerous rejections. Families are units which need local support, but they are still made up of individuals.

I believe all individuals are of value in the sight of God. It follows that we should do everything possible to ensure that the Wallys and the Sonias and the Alistairs should have the upbringing, the resources and the opportunities to allow them to choose to steer clear of delinquency and so develop their individual potential to the full for the common good. I also believe that all individuals are of equal value to God; Millie is as of much worth as other youngsters. This means that when Millie returns from prison, not just her mother but the rest of us must be ready to forgive, accept and befriend her.

Bibliography

D. Alton, 'Stopping the rot', *Third Way*, June 1994

R. Andry, *Delinquency and Parental Pathology*, Methuen, 1960

Sir Christopher Ball, *Start-Right. The Importance of Early Learning*, Royal Society of Arts, 1994

F. Beckett, *Call to Action*, Shaftesbury Society, 1989

J. Bowlby, *Child Care and the Growth of Love*, Pelican, 1953

R. Boyson, *Down with the Poor*, Churchill Press, 1971

J. Bradshaw & H. Holmes, *Living on the Edge*, Child Poverty Action Group, 1989

M. Bunting, 'Parents on the Front Line', *The Guardian*, 17 September 1991

C. Cannan, *Changing Families. Changing Welfare*, Harvester/Wheatsheaf, 1992

A. Christie, *Nemesis*, Paragon, 1993

R. Clapp, *Families at the Crossroads*, Inter-Varsity Press, 1993

M. Cockett & J. Tripp, cited in *The Guardian*, 8 February 1994

D. Dickinson, cited in *The Guardian*, 7 January 1994

D. Donnison, *Crime and Social Policy*, NACRO, 1995

M. Eastman, 'Reflections on young people and us', *Social Workers' Christian Fellowship Broadsheet*, Summer 1994

H. Eysenck, *The Inequality of Man*, Temple Smith, 1973

G. Gaskin with J. MacVeigh, *Gaskin*, Jonathan Cape, 1982

J. Gibbons with S. Thorpe & P. Wilkinson, *Family Support & Prevention*, HMSO, 1990

J. Groser, *Politics and Persons*, SCM Press, 1949

J. Heywood, *Children in Care*, Routledge & Kegan Paul, 1959

B. Holman, *The Evacuation. A Very British Revolution*, Lion Publishing, 1995.

B. Holman, *A New Deal for Social Welfare*, Lion Publishing, 1993

B. Holman, 'Diary', *The Guardian*, 12 June 1991

B. Holman, *Good Old George. The Life of George Lansbury*, Lion Publishing, 1990

B. Holman, *Putting Families First*, Macmillan Education, 1988

B. Holman, *'Not Like Any Other Home'. Herbert Smith and the Children's Home and Mission*, Campaign Literature, 1994

M. Hughes, *No Cake, No Jam. A War-time Childhood*, Heinemann, 1994

W. Hutton, 'The real price of poverty', *The Guardian*, 22 February, 1992

W. Hutton, 'Multitude of evils follows employment', *The Guardian*, 16 October 1992

C. Irvine, 'Diary', *The Guardian*, 14 December 1988

V. Jackopson, *From Prison to Pulpit*, Marshall Pickering, 1981

I. Kolvin with F. Miller, D. Scott, S. Katzanis & M. Fleeting, *Continuities of Deprivation*, Avebury 1991

E. Leach, cited by B. Holman, 1988

G. Lansbury, *My Life*, Constable, 1928

G. Lansbury, *My England*, Selwyn & Blount, 1934

S. Mapp, 'A Friend in Need', *Community Care*, 27 October 1994

M. Mayo, *Community and Caring*, St Martin's Press, 1994

C. Murray, *The Emerging British Underclass*, I.E.A., 1990.

R. Neale, *Bath. A Social History*, Routledge & Kegan Paul, 1981

E.Newson, *Video Violence and the Protection of Children*, University of Nottingham, 1994

T. O'Neill,*A Place Called Hope*, Basil Blackwell, 1981

K. Painter, cited in *The Guardian*, 2 March 1993

Pauline, *Families of Courage*, ATD Fourth World, 1984

C. Petrie, *The Nowhere Boys*, Saxon House, 1980

A. Phillips, 'Small steps in the right direction', *The Guardian*, 24 March 1991

A. Phillips, *The Trouble With Boys*, Pandora Press, 1993

K. Pringle, *The Needs of Children*, Hutchinson 1975

A. Raine, cited in *The Guardian*, 24 February 1994

R. Reiner, 'Crime and Control', *LSE Magazine*, Spring 1994

D. Riley & M. Shaw , *Parental Supervision and Juvenile Delinquency*, HMSO, 1985

D. Rose, 'The messy truth about Britain's violent youth', *The Observer*, 28 February 1993

P. Rosser, in *Deviance*, Workbook 5, Working with Children and Young People Course, Open University, 1990

M. Rutter & N. Madge, *Cycles of Deprivation*, Heinemann, 1976

R. Schaffer, 'Stable childhood in the midst of adult turbulence', *Child and Society*, Summer 1994

L.J. Schweinhart, D. Weikart & M. Lerner, 'Consequences of three Pre-School Curriculum Models through Age 15', *Early Education Research*, 1986

A. Shearer, 'Finding the way home', *The Guardian*, 23 December 1987

S. Shinman with S. Pope and S. Everitt, *Family Album*, Home-Start UK, 1994

Social Justice Strategies for National Review. The Report of the Commission on Social Justice, Vintage, 1994

D. Utting with J. Bright and C. Henricson, *Crime and the Family: Improving child- rearing and preventing delinquency*, Family Policy Studies Centre, 1993

W. Van der Eyken, *Home-Start: A Four Year Evaluation*, Home-Start Consultancy, 1990

M. Wadsworth, *The Roots of Delinquency*, Martin Robertson, 1979

D. West, *Delinquency: Its Roots, Careers and Prospects*, Heinemann, 1977

D. West & D.Farrington, *The Delinquent Way of Life*, Heinemann, 1977

M. Whitehead (ed.), *The Health Divide*, Health Education Council, 1987

R. Whitfield, 'Don't give in to pressure', *Community Care*, 24 January 1991

H. Wilson & G. Herbert, *Parents and Children in the Inner City*, Routledge & Kegan Paul, 1978

Women's Group on Public Welfare, *Our Towns: A Close-Up*, Oxford University Press, 1943.

B. Wright, *Possilpark Befriending Project Report*, Save the Children, 1993

Index

A

Alton, David 51
Andry, Robert 26

B

Ball Report 114, 118, 128
Beckett, Fran 148–49
Befriending
    examples of 176–80
    in the community 185–99
    resourceful friendship 175–76
    rules for befriending 200–203
    schemes 180–85
Bowlby, John 26, 37
Boyson, Rhodes 19
Bradshaw, Jonathan and
    Holmes, Hilary 64, 69
Bunting, Madeleine 38, 42

C

Children Act (1948) 178
Children Act (1989) 100, 126, 170
Christians 17–18, 149, 207, 212
Churches 110, 167, 210
Church of England Children's
    Society 7, 119
Clapp, Rodney 24
Commission on Social Justice
    207–208, 210–11
Custody 95–98

D

Day care
    day nurseries 108–109
    nursery education 109
    playgroups 109
    private nurseries 109
    value of 114–18
    voluntary provision 109–11

Delinquency
    and birth complications 43–44
    and boredom 89–90–157
    and conflict 90–91
    and day care 116
    and disruption 89, 91
    and family size 44
    and media 45–46
    and peer groups 44, 47
    and poverty 55–77, 85, 91
    and public forces 44–45, 92
    and public messages 48–53
    explanations of 18–21, 90–92
    extent of 15
    means of countering 207–214
    reasons for preventing 16–18
Dennis, Norman 35
Dickinson, David 58
Donnison, David 57

E

Eastman, Michael 153–54, 164–65
Education Reform Act (1988) 101
Ethnic minorities 14–15, 38–39,
    141
Eysenck, Hans 19

F

Family:
    as an idol 24
    broken families 32–36
    link with delinquency 22–24,
        26–28, 90–91
    part of fathers 26
    part of mothers 25–26
    positive features 37–40
Family centres 102–103, 119–29
Family Studies Policy Centre 131
FARE (Family Action in Rogerfield
    and Easterhouse) 168, 171
Friedman, Milton 50

G

Gaskin, Graham 86–87
Gibbons, Jane 102
Groser, Father John 212

H

Hackney 153
Handsworth Day Care Centre,
   Birmingham 111–14
Harrison, Margaret 139
Heywood, Jean 26
High/Scope Pre-School Project,
   USA 116–18
Holme Christian Care Centre,
   Bradford 167
Home-Start 139–45
Hughes, Marian 82–85
Hutton, Will 60, 209

I

Intermediate Treatment (IT)
   174–75

J

Jackopson, Vic 87–89
Juvenile crime *see* delinquency
Juvenile offenders:
   features of 13–16
   in institutions 95–98
   views of 78–89

K

Kolvin, Israel 26, 57

L

Lansbury, George 21, 60–61, 211–14
Lone parents 34–36, 72–73

M

Mapp, Susan 181–82
Mayo, Marjorie 169

Murray, Charles 19–20, 35

N

NCH Action for Children
   174–75
Neale, R.S. 20
Newpin 132–39
Newson, Elizabeth 47

O

O'Neill, Tom 176–80
Oregon Social Learning Centre,
   USA 131–32

P

Painter, Kate 38, 90, 180
Pauline 78–82
Patterson, Gerald 131–32
Petrie, Cairine 60, 95
Phillips, Angela 62, 135
Possilpark Befriending Project,
   Glasgow 183–85
Poverty
   action against 209–11
   and coping 73–77
   and day care 115
   examples of 64–69
   extent of 55
Prevention of delinquency
   and prediction 104–105
   better than custody 95–99
   by local authorities 99–103
   by neighbourhoods 105–107
   by voluntary bodies 103, 107
   reactive and positive prevention
      99
   targeting prevention 106–107
Pringle, Kellmer 28
Project 10, Newcastle-upon-Tyne
   164–167

R

Raine, Adrian 44
Reiner, Robert 54
Rose, David 97
Rosser, Philip 14
Rutter, Michael and Madge,
    Nicola 76

S

Salvation Army 178–82
Save the Children Fund 185
Schaffer, Rudolph 65
Schools 76, 102
Shaftesbury Society 129, 148
Shearer, Ann 132
St Gabriel's Family Centre,
    Walthamstow 124–26
Stigma 103–104, 105

T

Titmuss, Richard 6
Tot–Spot Crèche, Glasgow
    110–11
Townsend, Peter 209

U

Utting, David, 22, 33, 35, 57,
    101, 116

V

Van der Eyken, Willem 144
Volunteers 146–51

W

Wadsworth, Michael 33
Walcot Centre, Swindon
    119–24, 150
Walker Project, Newcastle-upon-
Tyne 161–62
Welfare state 19–21
West, Donald 152
West, Donald and Farrington,
    David 26, 33, 44, 57, 85, 90,
    104
White, Herbert 37, 45
Whitfield, Richard 36
Wiles, Dave 155–56, 157, 172,
188, 202
Wilson, Harriett and Herbert,
    Geoffrey 69–71, 74
Wright, B. 183

Y

Youth work:
    in the community 165–69
    ordinary clubs 154–60
    right features 170–172
    specialized youth work
160–165